JEWISH
HISTORICAL TREASURES

JEWISH HISTORICAL TREASURES

by Azriel Eisenberg

BLOCH PUBLISHING COMPANY
New York

To My Wife, Rose
on the Occasion of Our
Three-fold Celebration

ACKNOWLEDGMENTS

The author acknowledges with thanks and appreciation the permissions granted by the following institutions, publishers and individuals to reproduce the photographs in this book:

Am Oved, Tel Aviv, Page 146
American Jewish Historical Society, Waltham, Mass., Page 182
Archives Photographiques Caisse, Nationale des Monuments Historiques, Paris, Page 10
British Museum, London, Pages 6, 30, 32, 68, 77, 83, 95, 100
British Office of Information, New York, Pages 92, 150, 159
Brooklyn Museum, New York, Page 19
Buenos Aires Kehillah, Page 193
Buffalo and Erie Historical Society, Buffalo, N.Y., Page 174
Cambridge University Library, England, Page 26
Communita Israelitica di Roma, Italy, Page 66
Council of Concern for Soviet Jewry, Cleveland, Page 191
David deSola Pool, New York, Page 156
Frank J. Darmstaedter, New York, Pages 64, 65, 108, 168
Hebrew Union College—Jewish Institute of Religion, New York, Pages 109, 196, 197
Hebrew University, Jerusalem, Pages 79, 185
Israel Government Tourist Office, New York, Pages 36, 43, 70, 71
Israel National Museum, Jerusalem, Pages 30, 53
Israel Office of Information, New York, Pages 2, 8, 21, 28, 29, 32, 34, 40, 42, 44, 46, 47, 54, 56, 57, 62, 63, 138, 189, 195, 198
Istanbul Museum, Turkey, Pages 4, 14
Italian Office of Information, New York, Pages 38, 176, 177
Jewish Museum, New York (Ambur Hiken), Pages 132, 206
Jewish Publication Society of America, Philadelphia, Pages 58, 59
Jewish Theological Seminary Library, New York, Pages 24, 49, 73, 74, 76, 80, 81, 82, 83, 84, 89, 94, 102, 104, 107, 112, 114, 115, 116, 117, 118, 120. 124, 136, 137, 140
John Carter Brown Library, Providence, R. I., Page 144
Judah L. Cahn, New York, Page 191
Library of Congress, Washington, D.C., Pages 162, 164, 166, 167
Seymour M. Liebman, Miami, Florida, Page 134
Mikveh Israel Synagogue, Curacao, Foto Fischer, Pages 152, 153, 160, 161
Miriam Schaar Schoesinger, New York, Page 61
Mosad Bialik, Jerusalem, Page 130
Nathan Rappaport, New York, Pages 192, 193
Netherlands Information Office, New York, Pages 149, 154
New York Public Library, Pages 100, 172
Palestine Archeological Museum, Jerusalem, Page 16
Schocken Books, New York, Pages 22, 23, 32
Spanish Tourist Office, New York, Pages 90, 91, 98, 99
State Jewish Museum, Prague, Pages 86, 123, 128, 129, 142
Tomb of Unknown Jewish Martyr, Paris, Page 202
Yad Vashem, Jerusalem, 200, 201
Yivo, Yiddish Scientific Institute, New York, Pages 96, 126, 170, 206
Zionist Archives, New York, Pages 180, 181, 188
Zydowski Instytut Historyczny, Warsaw, Page 191

Contents

Preface

EACH age in Jewish history has left its peculiar artifacts. From the Biblical period there are archaeological treasures; from the early Middle Ages, manuscripts and incunabula; from the later Middle Ages, early printed books; and from more recent times, a wealth of monuments, documents and collectors' items. From among these I have chosen just over a hundred representative objects whose interest is primarily historical, with the aim of providing a visual survey of nearly four millennia in the life of the Jewish people.

For help and guidance in the compilation, I am especially indebted to Dr. Menahem Schmeltzer, Librarian, Jewish Theological Seminary of America; to Dr. A. M. Haberman, Librarian-emeritus, Schocken Library, Jerusalem; to Mrs. Sylvia Landress, Librarian, Zionist Archives and Library, and her associates; and to Dr. Elias Schulman, Librarian, Jewish Education Committee of New York.

I also acknowledge my thanks to the Lucius N. Littauer Foundation and to its president, Mr. Harry Starr, for assistance in making possible the collection of the photographs.

I am indeed deeply grateful to Mrs. Jacqueline L. Bergman for painstaking meticulous proofreading and intelligent corrections of the manuscript.

It is my hope that this kaleidoscopic presentation of history will serve to focus the attention of readers and students upon our colorful Jewish heritage, and to enrich the work of teachers as they impart the knowledge of our past and present.

AZRIEL EISENBERG

JEWISH
HISTORICAL TREASURES

Display at Ayelet Hashahar

Scene of the dig

Hazor

FIFTEENTH CENTURY B.C.E.

In Chapter 11 of the Book of Joshua, we learn that the city of Hazor had dominated the kingdoms of the Canaanites, Amorites, Hitties, Perizzites, Jebusites, and Hivites. At the waters of Merom (Kinneret) Joshua defeated all these kingdoms, allied to wage war on him. He took Hazor and put its king and its entire army to the sword.

Hazor was a strategic city. Seven miles north of Kinneret or Sea of Galilee, and about five miles southwest of Lake Huleh, the city dominated the road from Mesopotamia, Syria, and Anatolia to Egypt. It is mentioned in ancient Assyrian and Egyptian records. In the Bible it recurs often: in the days of the prophetess Deborah (Judges IV), who decisively defeated the Canaanites; of Solomon, who had it rebuilt as a royal city and garrison for his chariots (I Kings IX:15); of the Kings of Israel (II Kings XV:29), when it was conquered in 732 B.C.E., by the Assyrians; and in the days of the Hasmoneans (I Maccabees XI:63), as late as 147 B.C.E.

Since 1955 Hazor has been in the process of excavation under the leadership of Professor Yigael Yadin, who estimated that eight hundred years would be needed to dig up the 20-acre site completely. (Meggido was 15 acres.) The depth of the ruins is 40 meters.

Hazor seems to have been built originally in the fifteenth century B.C.E. The first three years of the excavation uncovered the remnants of a Canaanite sanctuary, with sacred stones, an altar, sacred vessels, and all the garnishings of a Canaanite temple.

There were also the bones of infants buried in jars, as well as tombs, cisterns, dwellings, and a potter's workshop. From the period of the Israelite occupation there were inscriptions, city walls, a city gate constructed by King Solomon, a residence and household relics, a two-story private house, and a silo for grain storage, along with sculpture, figurines, cult masks, seals, and ivories. The excavations were financed by James A. de Rothschild, and carried on by the Hebrew University under Professor Yadin's direction. The objects found are on display at a museum at nearby Ayelet Hashahar, the pioneering communal settlement or kibbutz of northern Galilee.

Note: All dates up to page 32 refer to the period before the Common or Christian Era (B.C.E.)

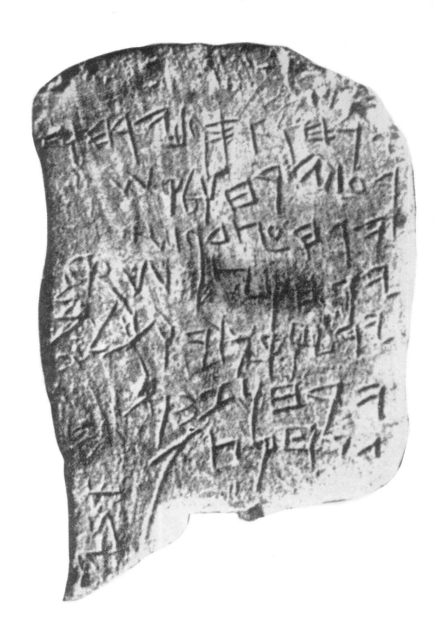

Gezer Calendar

The Gezer Calendar, dating back to the age of Saul or David (1030-1013), is believed to be the oldest existing inscription in early Hebrew writing. It is a small limestone tablet, 4½ inches high, 2¾ inches across, and ⅝ inch thick. The text reads:

> *Two months of olive harvesting*
> *two months of grain planting*
> *two months of late planting*
> *Month of pulling flax*
> *Month of barley harvest*
> *Month of harvest and festivity*
> *Two months of pruning (vines)*
> *Month of harvesting summer fruit*

This is evidently an agricultural calendar, probably used by a farmer or by an instructor. Discovered in 1908 at Gezer, twenty miles west-northwest of Jerusalem, by the archaeologist R. A. S. Macalister, it is now at the Museum of Istanbul, Turkey.

Black Obelisk of Shalmaneser III

One of the most impressive objects in the British Museum is the Black Obelisk of Shalmaneser III. It was found by Austen Henry Layard in 1840 during excavations of the Mount of Nimrod, near Mosul, Iraq, on the banks of the Euphrates River.

The monument concerns Shalmaneser III, who reigned over Assyria from 859 to 825 B.C.E. On each of its four sides are inscribed five scenes, each divided into four parts, showing the Assyrian king receiving tribute from the kings he had conquered, with an account of his victories. One side, which contains the only extant portrait of an Israelite king, is related to the Bible, although there is no direct mention of the event in the Scriptures.

In I Kings XIX:16 we are told that the prophet Elijah prepared Jehu for a rebellion against Joram, the wicked son of Ahab. In II Kings IX we read how Elisha anointed Jehu king of Israel. It is a chapter filled with intrigue, a palace revolution, bloodshed and murder, and with predictions of the decline of Israel: "In those days," reads verse 32, "the Lord began to cut Israel short."

Then the text refers to the Book of Chronicles of the Kings of Israel "for the rest of the acts of Jehu, and all that he did, and all his might." We do not have this book and do not know what was in it. But possibly the "lost" book may have contained an account of the events pictured by the Black Obelisk.

Jehu and his court are shown carved in figures as they appear to pay tribute to Shalmaneser III. Jehu is actually licking the dust before the Assyrian victor. The inscription reads: "The tribute of Jehu, son of Omri: silver, gold, a bowl of gold, a vase of gold, cups of gold, buckets of gold ... the balsam wood I received from him."

Horned altar found at Meggido

Megiddo

At Meggido, in the valley of Jezreel, two large compounds made up of stables accommodating from 450 to 500 horses were uncovered. The excavation, from 1925 to 1939, was begun by Professor James Henry Breasted of the University of Chicago. It was continued by Clarence S. Fisher of the University of Pennsylvania, and later by Mr. P. L. O. Guy of the Department of Antiquities of Palestine; it was financed by John D. Rockefeller, Jr.

Near the stables is heavy limestone hollowed out into troughs for grain. Between the mangers are large pillars, each with a hole used in tying the horses. There are also a parade ground, 180 feet square, its floor plastered with lime; a large cistern; and a passageway for the horses and their caretakers.

It was thought at first by members of the American expedition who made the discovery, that King Solomon had built these stables (see I Kings IX:17-19; X:26-29). In 1960, however, Professor Yigael Yadin of the Hebrew University rechecked and made new soundings of the excavation of Meggido; he concluded that although the city had been erected by Solomon as a defense outpost, the stables had probably been built about the time of Ahab (ca. 875-854), who had a force of some two thousands chariots.

Megiddo, or as it is known in Arabic, Tel el-Mutesellim ("Hill of the Commander"), was a center of military importance for thousands of years, and the city itself was most probably built because of its strategic location. It commanded the important pass leading from the coastal heights of Mt. Carmel to the plain of Jezreel. Through this narrow opening armies could travel between Egypt and Assyria. Thus it connected the continents of Africa and Asia, and was often the scene of severe conflicts. Control of Meggido meant control of the pass, and whoever controlled it was able to go freely between north and south. Because this city was the battleground of so many important struggles between nations, the writer of the New Testament Book of Revelation (XVI:16) chose the site for the final battle of God's armies with the forces of evil. He called it Armaggedon, a word compounded of the Hebrew word *har* (mountain) and Megiddo.

The Moabite Stone

CA. 840 B.C.E.

This stone or stele commemorating the victories of King Mesha of Moab over Israel (II Kings III:6) contains more than 30 lines of carved writing which connect it closely with the biblical story. It is thus of historical, religious, and linguistic importance.

In II Samuel VIII:2, there is an account of how David subjugated Moab, which lay east of the Jordan near the northern shores of the Dead Sea. After the division of the kingdom during the days of Omri (887-876) and his son Ahab (ca. 875-854), Moab was still a vassal of Israel, as is clear from the biblical narrative in II Kings III:4 and also from the inscription on the Moabite Stone. The account of Mesha's revolt in the Bible differs from the inscription in several respects, including the date. But the text on the stone (in the first person singular) confirms the biblical narrative, and the contradictions are minor. It sheds light on the relations of ancient Israel with her neighbors and mentions many cities and places found in the Bible.

The Stone (4' x 2' x 1') was accidentally discovered in the summer of 1868 by a German missionary, F. A. Klein, at Diban (the biblical Dibon), thirteen miles east of the Dead Sea. Fortunately a reproduction of its contents had been made before it was broken up by hostile and superstitious bedouins. Most of the pieces were recovered and reassembled and are now at the Museum of the Louvre in Paris.

11

The Signet Seals

Seals were used in biblical days to enclose and sign documents and to indicate ownership. Seals discovered from those early days therefore constitute an important source of early Hebrew inscriptions.

From I Kings XXI:8; Isaiah VIII:16, XXIX:11; and Jeremiah XXXII:10 ff., it is clear how essential it was to give titles to property and authentication to letters and other documents. At present there are anywhere from 100 to 200 such seals extant, some of them dating from the seventh to the fourth century B.C.E. They are carved of hard semi-precious stones such as cornelian, jaspar, agate, onyx, jade, and opal. They vary in shape, although most of them are oval or scarab-shaped with the back slightly vaulted. Some were pierced through so as to be worn on a string; some were set in rings.

Perhaps the most impressive of the early Hebrew seals is one made of jaspar in the shape of a scarab, which shows a roaring lion and is inscribed at the top *l'shm,* an abbreviation for "belonging to Shema," and at the bottom *bdyrbm,* for "servant of Jeroboam." Shema, the owner, was a minister of King Jeroboam II (785-745). The seal is almost two inches long, slightly over an inch wide, and two-thirds of an inch thick. The lion was a favorite motif on seals. Also often used were winged creatures (cherubim, seraphim) and various other animals.

The seal of Shema was found on the ancient site of Megiddo (Tel el-Mutesellim) in 1904. It was kept by the Turkish Sultan at Constantinople, and later at the Museum of the Antiquities in the same city; regrettably, it is now lost.

The signet of Jaazaniah is a scarab-shaped seal made of onyx, black banded in white; it dates back to about 600. In its center is engraved a fighting cock; on the top is the word *ly'znhyu,* for "belonging to Jaazaniah," and at the bottom *bdhmlk,* for "servant of the King." It is generally assumed that the owner was a captain in the Judean army at the time of Gedaliah, son of the Maachathite, commander of Mizpah, mentioned in II Kings XXV:23 and in

Jeremiah XL:13. The signet was discovered by archaeologists of the Pacific School of Religion, Berkeley, California.

The seal of Hoshayahu is characteristic of the later Judean period, from the seventh century on, after pictorial representations had been abolished in the religious reformation instituted by Josiah (621). It can be seen that this seal has no pictorial representation, but is inscribed in flowing early Hebrew script. It reads on top *lhsh'yh,* "belonging to Hoshayahu" and on the bottom *bn shimyh,* for "son of Shalmiyahu." It is now in the private collection of the noted scholar and antiquarian, Dr. A. Reifenberg, in Jerusalem.

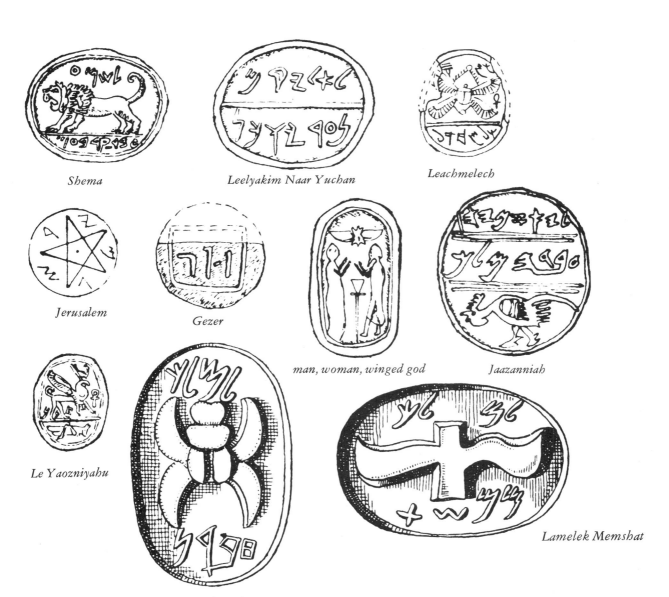

Shema

Leelyakim Naar Yuchan

Leachmelech

Jerusalem

Gezer

man, woman, winged god

Jaazanniah

Le Yaozniyahu

Lamelek Hebron

Lamelek Memshat

הנקבה . וזה . היה . דבר . הנקבה . בעוד
הגרזן . אש . אל . רעו . ובעוד . שלש . אמת . להכ   קל . אש . ק
רא . אל . רעו . כי . חית . זדה . בצר . מימן `   ובים . ה
נקבה . הכו . החצבם . אש . לקרת . רעו . גרזן . על . גרזן . וילכו
המים . מן . המוצא . אל . הברכה . במאתים . ואלף . אמה . ומ[א]
ת . אמה . היה . נבה . הצר . על . ראש . החצב[ם]

Inscription in modern alphabet

Siloam Inscription

CA. 700 B.C.E.

This, the oldest carved stone inscription in early Hebrew, was originally located in the Pool of Siloam in Old Jerusalem, about nineteen feet from the entrance on the south side of the tunnel and five feet above the ground. It is about 29 feet long and 15 feet high. The tunnel, which connects the spring of Gihon of biblical days (now called the Virgin Spring) with the Pool of Siloam, is over 1,700 feet long; a direct line between the two points would be about 1,090 feet. The tunnel was built by Hezekiah, King of Judea, who, according to II Chronicles XXXII:30, "stopped the upper spring of the waters of Gihon, and brought them straight down on the west side of the city of David." (References to Hezekiah's excavation of the tunnel also occur in II Kings XX:2; Isaiah XXII:11; and Ben Sirah XLVIII:17.) It is assumed that the tunnel was part of the preparations by the Judean kingdom in anticipation of Sennacherib's invasion in 701 B.C.E. For some mysterious reason Sennacherib's forces withdrew, and Jerusalem was saved.

The inscription reads: "The completing of the piercing through. And this is the story of the piercing through. While the stone-cutters were swinging their axes, each towards his fellow; and while there were yet three cubits to be pierced through, there was heard the voice of a man calling to his fellow, for there was a crevice on the right... And on the day of the piercing through, the stone-cutters struck through each to meet his fellow, axe against axe. Then ran the water from the Spring to the Pool, for twelve hundred cubits was the height of the rock above the head of the stone-cutters."

From this it is clear that the Siloam tablet was affixed at the point where the two gangs of diggers met; one had started from the pool, the other from the spring at Gihon. This was a masterly feat of engineering. The deviation in digging the tunnel was probably deliberate to avoid disturbing the tombs of the kings.

The inscription was found by a youth on a summer day in 1880. It is at the museum of Istanbul.

15

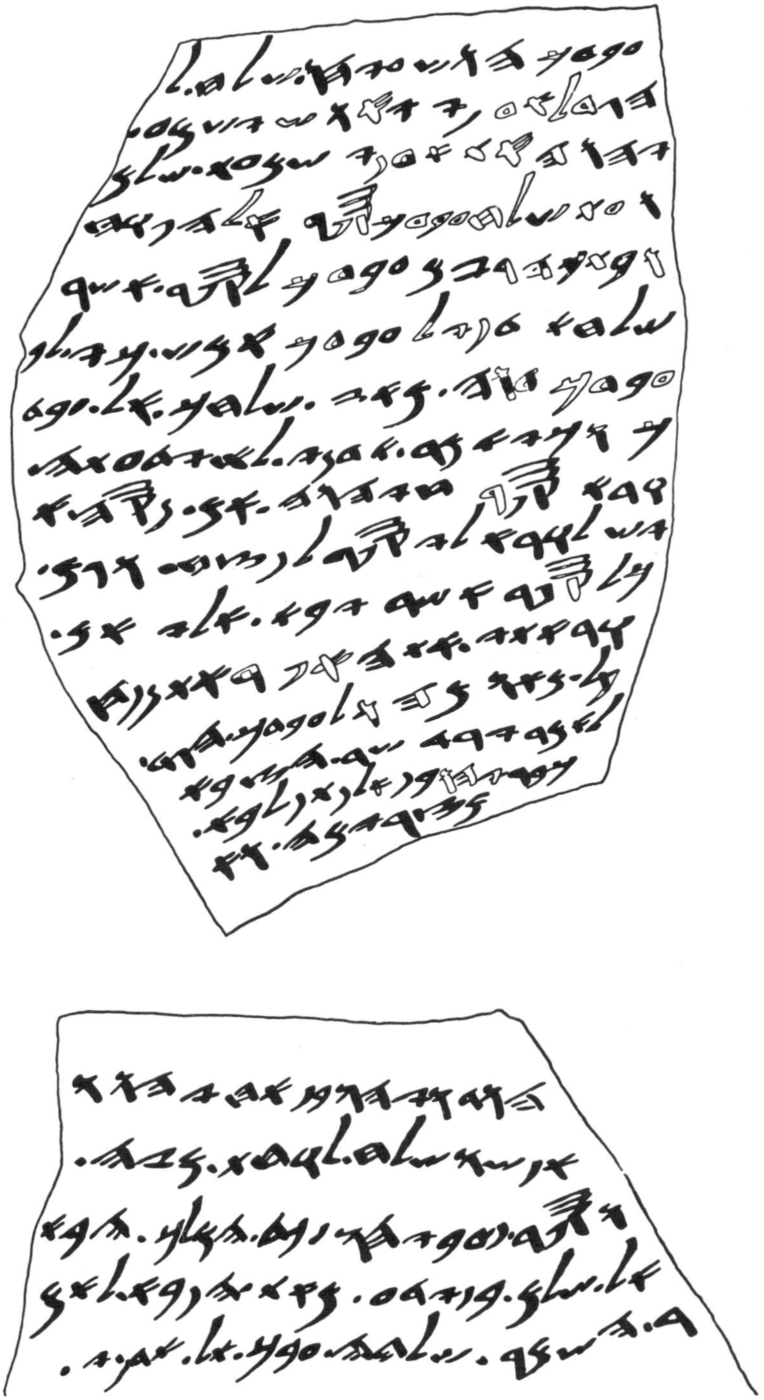

Lachish Letters

589 B.C.E.

The Lachish Letters contain the oldest known Hebrew inscription on potsherds or broken pieces of pottery, known as *ostraca* (singular, *ostracon*), used for writing letters much as we use note paper today. The letters, eighteen in all, were found in the ruins of a small room under a gate-house tower that was part of the fortified wall of the southern Judean city of Lachish (called by the Arabs Tel-el-Duweir), in the Negev, not far from Beersheba.

The Lachish Letters date back to the days of Jeremiah and Zedekiah, or around 590-586. They belong to the period that witnessed the end of the Kingdom of Judah. Mention of the episode is made in Jeremiah XXXIV:7: "Then Jeremiah the prophet spoke all these words unto Zedekiah in Jerusalem, when the king of Babylon's army fought against all the cities of Judah that were left, against Azekah, for these remained of the cities of Judah as fortified cities."

The letters, which were written with a wood or reed pen in ink, were apparently sent to Yaosh, the city's military governor, from surrounding outposts. The name of the sender is Hoshayahu. The language is similar to the Hebrew of the Bible.

Scholars assume that the script with its flowing penmanship, the spelling, the use of a dot to divide the words, the splitting up of words at the end of a line, and so on, are the same as in scrolls on which the biblical books were written in those days.

Based on the findings of these letters, Professor N. Y. Tursinai (Torczyner) of the Hebrew University, Jerusalem, has reconstructed a fascinating story of conflict, treason, and trial in *The Lachish Letters,* published by Oxford University in 1938.

The letters were discovered in 1935 and subsequent years by James L. Starkey, who headed the Wellcome Archaeological Expedition of England; they are now at the Archaeological Museum in Jerusalem.

17

Elephantine Papyri

FIFTH CENTURY B.C.E.

Not far from the noted Aswan Dam in southern Egypt is the site of the ancient island city of Elephantine and its twin community, Syene. From the first both cities were active trading posts (in fact, the word *Syene* means "trading post"). The name Syene occurs twice in the Book of Ezekiel (XXIX:10, XXX:6), where the biblical writer uses the phrase "from Migdol to Syene" as a figurative expression meaning all of Egypt.

At some time during the seventh or sixth century, an Egyptian Pharaoh appears to have placed a Jewish garrison at Elephantine to guard the frontier against Cush (the present-day Sudan) and to collect taxes on goods brought in from the south. Just where these Jews came from, and why they were sent there, is still uncertain; but their presence is attested by papyrus documents dating to the fifth century. In these papyri Elephantine is referred to as "Yeb the Fortress." They are written in Aramaic, the same language used in parts of the Books of Ezra and Nehemiah. The most surprising discovery in connection with the Elephantine papyri is that the community had a temple of its own, despite the injunction in the Book of Deuteronomy that the one place in which the Jews were to offer sacrifice was the Temple at Jerusalem.

In the year 410 B.C.E. the Temple at Elephantine was destroyed by the Egyptians. In 407 a letter was addressed to Bagoas, Persian governor of Judea, asking him to use his influence to have the ruined temple rebuilt. From the mention in the same letter of the sons of Sanballat's bitter opponent, it was possible for the first time to date the reign of Nehemiah as governor of Judea.

Another document known as the Passover Papyrus is dated from Jerusalem, 419 B.C.E., some twelve years before the Letter to Bagoas. It bears the signature of a certain Hananiah, who is believed by most scholars to have been a brother of Nehemiah himself, mentioned in the Book of Nehemiah I:2. The letter speaks of an official command by the king of Persia to have the Jews observe what from the context appears almost certainly to be the Feast of the Passover, though there are worm holes in the papyrus where the words "Passover lamb" and "unleavened bread" are presumed to have been written.

The Elephantine papyri were purchased in Egypt by an American, Charles Edwin Wilbour, in 1893; they are currently located in the Brooklyn Museum, N.Y.C. Other collections are found in England and Germany.

The Temple Area

CA. 961-920 B.C.E.; CA. 480 B.C.E.;
73-4 B.C.E.

Now that Old and New Jerusalem are united, it is easy and convenient to walk by foot from New Jerusalem to the Temple Area on Mount Moriah. According to Jewish tradition, it is this mount to which Abraham brought his son Isaac for an offering to God. Here, it is believed, Jacob dreamt of the ladder leading to heaven. Here were built the Temples of Solomon, Zerubbabel and Herod. According to the Jewish Encyclopedia (Volume XII, page 100), the probable site of the Temple was just west of the Mosque of Omar.

Shiningly resplendent in the very middle of the Temple Area— called in Arabic *Harem es-Sharif*, the "Venerable or August Sanctuary"—is the Mosque of Omar, named after the Caliph Omar who, it is alleged, first built a shrine there in 638. When the Crusaders conquered Jerusalem, in the eleventh century, they converted the sanctuary into a church and called it Templum Domini (the Knights Templar derived their name from it). In 1187 Saladin drove out the Crusaders and reconverted it into a Moslem shrine— the third most sacred in Islam after Mecca and Medina.

The Mosque is octagonal in shape with gilded capitals; it is set with brown, black, blue, green and mother-of-pearl mosaics on a gold background. Around the walls are inscriptions in Arabic from the Koran as well as names of the donors. Inside at the center of the gleaming, splendid structure is the Rock, in Arabic "Sakhra." Overarching the structure is a magnificent, colorful mosaic dome, hence the name, Dome of the Rock.

The Moslems believe that Mohammed ascended heavenward from this Rock on his mysterious steed Al Borak, and that his footprint is impressed at the southwest corner of the Rock. Some Jews have maintained that this rock is the *Even Hashettiyah*—which in Jewish tradition is the Foundation Stone marking the center of the earth. Some believe it may have been the sacrificial altar set up by King David on the threshing floor of Araunah the Jebusite. David's offering of sacrifices averted the plague from the Children of Israel (II Samuel, Chapter 24). Scholars opine that the bronze altar of the Temple was probably situated on the Rock. However that may be, the persistency of the memory of the sacredness of the Rock connects it most likely with an ancient shrine of Biblical times.

20

The Rock is overhung by a canopy and surrounded by a wooden railing. Its rise above the marble pavement ranges from four feet nine-and-a-half inches to one foot. From north to south it measures fifty-six feet and from east to west forty-two feet. Beneath the Rock there is a small cave hewn out of the rock believed by the Moslems to be inhabited by the souls of the dead. There is a Jewish legend that the sacred vessels of the Temple and the treasures of the Kings of Judah were stored there after the destruction in 70 C. E.

The Rock

Temple area

Coins: Beka; Yehud; Maccabean

BEKA

FIFTH CENTURY B.C.E.

The use of minted metal coins originated in the seventh century B.C.E. At first they were used as they are today, as tokens of value in place of direct barter. Later bits of precious metals, especially gold or silver, weighing a specific amount, were used; these are mentioned in Genesis XXIV:22 and Exodus XXXVIII:26. The *beka* belongs to the latter part of the fifth century B.C.E., or the period of Ezra and Nehemiah.

YEHUD COIN
FOURTH CENTURY B.C.E.

The earliest coin in Judea dates from the fourth century B.C.E. On the obverse side (i.e., facing the observer) is a full-length figure (a Greek god?) seated on a winged wheel and holding a hawk or eagle. Above appear the character *Y H D* in early Hebrew script. This is the Aramaic form of *Yehudah* or *Judah,* which was the designation of the province of Judea in the Persian period as found in Ezra V:1, 8. This ancient coin is in the collection at the British Museum.

MACCABEAN COINS

John Hyrcanus (135-104) of the Maccabean dynasty was the first Jewish ruler to issue coins stamped with his own name. Although not beautiful, these coins are of good workmanship. They are small, but the lettering is clear; no human figures appear on them, in obedience to the Second Commandment: "Thou shalt make no graven image." Instead, there are flowers, vines, cornucopias, and the like.

COIN OF JOHN HYRCANUS
(1 3 5 - 1 0 4   B.C.E.)

Obverse: wreath of laurel around the inscription "Jehohanan the High Priest and the Council of the Jews;" Reverse: two jugates, horns of plenty, and pomegranate.

COIN OF ALEXANDER JANNAEUS
(1 0 3 - 7 6   B.C.E.)

Obverse: half-opened flower. Inscribed "Jehonathan the King." (Yanai, the Hebrew form for Janneus, is an old abbreviation of Jehonathan.) Reverse: an anchor to show that Judea has become a naval power, and the Greek inscription, "of King Alexander."

23

מונע ומעשהג ושור מלכו׃ כי מקוה זדרן חטא ומיקורית

יבוע זמה׃ עלקיפילא לבושא נגעה ויכהיעד כלי׃

כסא גאים הפך להים ותשב ענוים תחתם׃ עקבת גוים

טומטם להים ושרשם שר ארץ קעקעי ותסס מארץ

ותשם ותובת צארץ זכרם׃ לא נאוה לאיש זדרן נאות

אף לילוד אשה׃ זרע נכבד מה זרע לאנוש וזרע נקלה

עוברי מצוה׃ בין אחים ראשם נכבד וירא להים

גשזד. נמדי ורש תפארכתם אית להים אין לבזות

ואין לכבד כל על מושר ושופט נכדרן

גידל לרא להים׃ עבד מושריל חכם ועבים

יועונן׃ לעיתתחכם לבד חנען למב

צדכה׃ טוב עובד ועתישחן על עכבד יס מתנו

בני בעטה כבד נפשך ותך לך ט ריו לא בדלי

מדשיע נפש מייצדיקטו ומי יכבד מקלה נפשו׃

יש דלינכבד בגלל שכלן ויש נכבד בגלל עשר

נכבד בעשרו איכסה תקלה בעינו אריה׃ ובכד

בדלאתו בעשרו מתכבר יתר ונקלה בעשרו בדלאתו

נקלה יותר׃ חכצ דיל תשא ראשו ובין נדיבים תשובנו

אל תהלל אדם בתארו ואל תתעב ארס יכ מי במראהו

אליל בעטף דבירה וראש תנובות פריה שנעשה אלר

תהל ולא תקלס במרישהירם׃ כי כלאות מעשי ונעש

אלך פעלו׃ רבים נדכאים ושבו על כ אבל על

ילב שטו צנף׃ רבים נשאים כלל ויד ונתשפלו אח

ובס נכבדים נתנו בד׃ בטרט תחיר אתסלף בקר

לפניט ואחר תסף י בני להשכיל דבר טרם תשמע

ובתוך שיחה אלתדבר׃ באין עצבה לא תאחר ובדב זדיס

אלתקואס׃ בני למה תרבה עשקך ואץ עלהיבות לא עקהי

בני אס לא תרוץ לא תגיע ואס לא תבקש לא תמצא׃

Apocryphal Book of Ben Sira

SECOND CENTURY B.C.E.

The Apocrypha is a collection of fourteen books, or parts of books, written during the last two centuries before and the first century of the Common Era. They are not included in the Holy Scriptures, but appear in the Catholic version of the Bible, and up until the printing of the King James Version were also found in Protestant Bibles.

The word Apocrypha means "things that are hidden." When the Holy Scriptures were sealed, those not canonized were hidden away or withdrawn from general use. Among the "hidden" was the book of Joshua Ben Sira (or Sirach), also known as Ecclesiasticus, which in Latin means "the Church book" or "pertaining to the Church."

Ben Sira was a scribe, i.e., one learned in Torah, and a teacher who probably lived in Jerusalem. About 180 B.C.E. he wrote down his teachings on ethics and religion, a work of fifty-one chapters, of the same type as the "wisdom literature" in the Book of Proverbs. Some fifty years later his grandson translated the book into Greek, in which form it came down through the centuries. The Jews made no attempt to preserve any of the books of the Apocrypha, although Ben Sira and other books were quoted in the Talmud and in later Jewish writings.

It was not until 1896 that fragments of the original Hebrew manuscript were found by Solomon Schechter in the Cairo Genizah, the depository or storage place for sacred Hebrew writings worn out from long use. The Genizah has yielded about two-thirds of the Hebrew text, a page of which is here reproduced. It is part of the Genizah Collection of the Jewish Theological Seminary in New York City.

25

Nash Papyrus

SECOND CENTURY B.C.E.

Up until discovery of the Dead Sea Scrolls in 1947, the Nash Papyrus (so named because it was acquired by Mr. W. L. Nash) was the oldest Hebrew text known. It contains a somewhat damaged inscription of the Ten Commandments, in a form that follows in part the versions in Chapter XX of Exodus and Chapter V of Deuteronomy, together with the *Shema* (Deuteronomy VI:4). Its contents suggest that the Nash Papyrus, consisting of four fragments, may have been part of a liturgical collection or text used for worship. If so, it is the oldest fragment of its kind extant.

It is of special interest that the sixth and seventh commandments appear in reverse order. Moreover, the *Shema* is introduced by a phrase, "And these are the statutes and ordinances which Moses commanded to the Children of Israel when they went out of the land of Egypt." The same phrase is used as introduction to the *Shema* in the Septuagint, Greek translation of the Bible, but is not found in the authoritative traditional (Masoretic) Hebrew text. The phrase "The House of Bondage," is deleted; was it because it may have been composed in Egypt and they did not want to give offense?

The Nash Papyrus has been dated by William F. Albright, leading biblical archaeologist, to the Maccabean period (168 B.C.E.). Other scholars date it to the first and second centuries C.E.

It was presented by W. L. Nash, who acquired it in Egypt in 1903, to the library of Cambridge University in England, where it is treasured to this day.

Facsimile

27

Amphitheatre
The Breakwater

Caeserea

Some 50 miles northwest of Jerusalem and 25 south of Haifa on the shore of the Mediterranean, lies Caeserea, built by Herod in 10 B.C.E. Herod, King of Judea, was a cruel tyrant but at the same time a great builder. He rebuilt the Temple in Jerusalem, and also a splendid seaport which he named in honor of the Roman emperor Caesar Augustus—hence Caeserea.

To this day may be seen the huge limestone blocks sunk into the water to make a breakwater. Ruins of an aqueduct which carried fresh water from the slopes of Mount Carmel are also still extant.

Most impressive, however, is the Roman amphitheatre that could accommodate thousands of spectators. This semi-circular open air theatre, while still littered with broken columns of marble and once proud capitals, presents a beautiful sight and is the scene of concerts in the autumn by world renowned virtuosos. In the theatre wall was found a stone bearing the names of the Roman emperor Tiberius and the governor of Judea, Pontius Pilate, he who ordered the crucifixion of Jesus.

Other ruins in Caeserea are remains of some impressive statuary, 4th-7th century synagogues, fortifications and buildings erected by the Crusaders, the Byzantines, and the Romans. Most noteworthy is a hippodrome, not yet cleared, which held, it is estimated, 20,000 spectators.

Today Caeserea is a sportsman's paradise, boasting a beautiful hotel, golf links, and other facilities for vacationists who can afford the highest tariffs in Israel for a holiday or summer resort.

Statuary

Uzziah inscription

Limestone Ossuary

Set Shearim Ossuaries

Memorial Tablet From the Ossuary of King Uzziah

FIRST CENTURY B.C.E.

An ossuary was a receptacle of wood, clay, or limestone in which the bones of the dead were placed for burial. In the days of the Second Temple the dead were laid first on a shelf in the family vault, hewn in the rock on land belonging to the family. When room had to be made for other bodies there was a secondary burial in an ossuary. Usually ossuaries were ornamented with six-pointed stars, rosettes, floral and other conventional patterns, and inscribed with the name of the deceased. Such an inscription was found on an ossuary at the Russian church on the Mount of Olives. It reads: "Hither were brought the bones of Uzziah, King of Juda. Do not open." The inscription is an interesting example of Jewish writing of the period.

Uzziah (or Azariah) reigned as king of Judea for fifty-two years, in the latter part of the eighth century. From II Kings XV and II Chronicles XXVI we can reconstruct the story of his life. Evidently a capable king, he was a soldier, statesman, and agrarian reformer. He subdued the Philistines and Ammonites, and successfully followed a policy of peace with the kingdom of Israel and the rest of his neighbors. He had wells dug for the use of herdsmen in watering their flocks, and provided irrigation for vineyards and grainfields. During his reign Elath, the port at the head of the Gulf of Aqaba, was restored—indicating an attempt to carry on commerce with surrounding countries. Uzziah secured the road to this remote port with a series of strongholds, manned by well-trained troops.

In the latter part of his life King Uzziah was struck with leprosy, which compelled him to withdraw from public affairs. According to II Chronicles XXVI:16-23, the disease was a punishment from God because "he went into the Temple of the Lord to burn incense upon the altar of incense." This was usurpation of the function of the priests, and a transgression of the law. His corpse therefore was not laid to rest in the royal mausoleum, but in the "cemetery which belongs to the kings." Later, probably between the beginning of the first century B.C.E. and the end of the first century C.E., his remains were transferred to the ossuary on which the above inscription was incised. The discovery was made by Professor E.L. Sukenik of the Hebrew University.

Coins From the First Jewish Revolt Against Rome

66-70 C.E.

Most famous of all Jewish coins is the *shekel* struck during the revolt against Rome. These coins announced to the world that Judea was independent of Roman rule. The shekel was of silver and was used for paying dues to the Temple. The picture is the obverse side, inscribed "Shekel of Israel," and dated *shin beth* or "year two" (i.e. 67 C.E.); it shows a wine cup. The other side is inscribed in Hebrew "Jerusalem the Holy" with a stem from which hang three pomegranates. Similar designs are seen on the half-shekel.

On bronze coins of the second year we see an amphora (jar) and the inscription, "Year Two"; on the reverse, a vine branch and the inscription, "Freedom of Zion."

The tragic end of the revolt is portrayed on the famous "Judea Capta" coin. The obverse shows a bust of the Emperor Vespasian, the inscription, "Year Two"; on the reverse, a vine branch and the the legend "Judea Capta," and "SC" (for "Senatus Consulto").

COIN OF ANTIGONUS MATTATHIAS
(40-37 B.C.E.)

Obverse: double cornucopia. Inscribed "Mattathias the High Priest and the Council of the Jews." Obverse in Hebrew. Reverse: ivy wreath. Inscribed in Greek, "of King Antigonos."

Street leading to wall

The Western (Wailing) Wall

70 C.E.

The site most hallowed to the Jewish people is the western remnant of the wall that once surrounded the Temple Mount. The main part, and most ancient section of the wall nineteen or twenty-one huge rows of stone, lies buried in the earth. Tradition has it that these stones are the foundation of the Temple set by King David. The stones immediately above the ground belong to the days of the First and Second Temples; the rest were added in later times. Opinions differ as to just when they were added. Some maintain that the first four rows above the bottom nine were built by Bar Kokhba; others say that they were erected by Emperor Hadrian. Above these are rows of stone blocks which date from the time of Arab domination. The height of the wall is 18 meters, or 59½ feet. At each of the two ends of the wall the Arabs have added five rows of stone in recent years.

In front of the Western Wall is a narrow quadrangle, measuring 28 meters or 91.8 feet in length, and 3.60 meters or 11.8 feet in width. On one side the square is closed off by the courtyards of the Moslems. For the Western Moroccan Moslems the houses and yards around the wall constitute a holy site, whose ownership may not be transferred.*

The Arab Moslems never regarded the Western Wall and its immediate surroundings as holy, but subjected the place to the basest and most humiliating usage. They would pass through the square mounted on asses carrying garbage and manure, and molest the Jews who stood there in prayer. Once the city council decided to run the sewer of the Old City through the square before the Western Wall, and it was only through the protests of the Jews that the plan was frustrated.

Until the year 5655 (1894), the square and alleys leading to the wall were not paved. In the winter of that year, through the efforts of the Jews, the city council was persuaded to pave narrow paths leading to the Western Wall and to the passage before it with large, smooth stones. The Wall is in Old Jerusalem, in what was formerly the Jordanian sector of the Holy City.

Since June, 1967 this situation was changed.

35

Tomb of Rachel

Scene of the interior

Cave of Machpela

The Tomb of Rachel at Bethlehem

In Genesis 35:18-20 we read of how Rachel breathed her last after giving birth to Benjamin, and of how Jacob buried her on the road to Ephrath—now Bethlehem: "Over her grave Jacob set up a pillar; it is the pillar at Rachel's grave to this day." In I Samuel 10:2, on the other hand, we read that the grave was to the north of Jerusalem, bordering on the land of the tribe of Benjamin. Whatever the historical fact may be, Jewish tradition has long accepted the version found in Genesis, and today the spot remains a popular shrine, as it has been for both Jews and Moslems throughout a millennium and more. The tomb that marks the spot has undergone many transformations. The present structure, built some centuries ago, was restored in 1841 by Sir Moses and Lady Judith Montefiore, and the tomb at Ramsgate, England, where they are buried is modeled after it.

Many legends and superstitions are connected with the tomb of Rachel. The throngs of visitors are especially numerous during the month of Ellul and the Ten Days of Penitence, when Jews traditionally visit the graves of their forebears.

The Cave of Machpelah in Hebron

When Sarah died, it was Abraham's wish to bury her in the cave of Machpelah in Kiriath-arba, or what is now Hebron. The twenty-third chapter of Genesis tells of the negotiations and the final purchase of the field containing it from Ephron the Hittite, for a sum of four hundred shekels of silver: "And the field with its cave passed from the children of Heth to Abraham, as a burial site."

Abraham himself, and Isaac, Rebecca, and Jacob, were all likewise buried there (Genesis 25:8-9; 49:29; 50:1-12). Throughout their long history this has been one of the shrines most revered by Jews, and it is surrounded by countless legends, to which the Moslems — who likewise revere the Patriarchs — have contributed their share.

The Arch of Titus in Rome

70 C.E.

The Emperor Titus ruled in Rome from 79 to 81 C.E. Son of Vespasian, the conqueror of Jerusalem, he led the siege against the Holy City, destroyed the capital, and burned the Temple in the year 70. It has been estimated that some 1,100,000 Jews were killed during the war with Judea, and that some 97,000 were taken prisoner after the fall of Jerusalem. On the return of Titus to Rome there was a triumphal procession, headed by two captured heroes, John of Gischala and Simon bar Giora, and including seven hundred picked Jewish soldiers. Two triumphal arches were erected in honor of the emperor's victory, and one of these still stands in the Roman Forum, about twenty yards from the Tiber. One side faces the Colosseum, the other the Forum. The inside of the arch contains three bas-reliefs, one of which shows Roman soldiers, weaponless and crowned with laurels, carrying the sacred objects from the Temple as spoils of victory. The objects depicted include two tablets fastened on staffs, the seven-branched menorah, and the golden table, upon which lie the sacred trumpets used to summon worshipers to the Temple.

Through the ages, Jews have observed the tradition of never passing under the arch.

The bas-relief

The Dead Sea Scrolls
(The Book of Isaiah)

CA. 100 B.C.E.-100 C.E.

The Dead Sea Scrolls now in possession of the State of Israel were discovered in a cave in the Judean desert. The scrolls are of coarse animal hide, with the writing on the outside of the skin. The parchment is ruled and the text appears under rather than over the line. Even now a Jewish scribe or copyist writes a Torah (the Five Books of Moses) in the same way.

The Dead Sea Scrolls were found wrapped in linen cloth. Some of the wrappings have hemmed borders; others are woven with blue stripes. They were probably made especially for the purpose of wrapping the scrolls.

The beautifully formed writing shows that the men who prepared the text were scholars. Wherever they were not sure about spelling, grammar, or sentence structure, they marked the place by putting dots above and beneath.

One of the best preserved of the manuscripts is that of the Book of Isaiah shown here. The oldest complete copy of any book from the Bible known today, it includes all sixty-six chapters. It evidently saw good service, for many selections torn by frequent handling were repaired with small strips of leather, and in places the ink is faded. In spelling, the words differ slightly from the traditional Hebrew of the Masoretic texts but the number and order of chapters and verses in the scroll correspond to the book we use today.

Much of the interest and value of the scrolls is for biblical scholars and for specialists interested in the history of the alphabet, of writing, of the development of language in general, and of the Hebrew language in particular.

Discovered accidentally in 1947 by an Arab bedouin at Ain Feshkha in the wilderness of Judea near the Dead Sea, a number of the scrolls were acquired by Dr. Eliezer Sukenik and his son, General Yigael Yadin, now professor at the Hebrew University. The seven scrolls owned by the State of Israel are specially housed in a part of the Israel National Museum called the Shrine of the Book. The Museum is located near the campus of the Hebrew University in Jerusalem.

Jars in which scrolls were preserved

41

חחצוצרות תהויינה פרויעת לנצח אנשי הקלע עד כלותם להשליך שבע

פעמים ואחר יתקעו להם חנוחנום בחצוצרות המשוב ובאו ליד המערכה

הראשונה להתעצב על מעמדם ותקעו הכוהנים בחצוצרות המקרא וידא

שלושה דגלי ביניים מן השערים ועמדו ברו המערכות ולוים אנשי חונב

ביניים ומשמאיל ותקעו הכוהנים בחצוצרות קול מרורר ידי סדר מלחמה

והראשים ויהיו נעמדום לסדריהם איש למעמדו וכעומדם שלושה סדרים

ותקעו להם חנוחנום תרועה שנית קול נוח וסמוך יהיו מגשעעד קורבכ

למערכת האויב ונטו ידם בכלא המלחמה וחנוחנום יריעו כשש חצוצרות

החלולום קול חד טרוד לנצח מלחמה וחלויים וכל עם השוטרות יריעו

קול אחד תרועת מלחמה גדולה להמס לב אויב ועם קול החד...עד יצא

וריות המלחמה להנגל חללום קול השוטרות יחישו וכה   יתן וחדו

חנוחנום פריעת קול חד טרוד לנצח יהיו מלחמה עד השליוכב למערכת

האויב שבע נעמים ואחר יתקעו להם חנוחנום בחצוצרית המשוב

קול נוח פרוור סמוך בסור חוה יתקעו ׃   ינום לשלשת הדגלים ועם

חטל הראישון וריעו ׃   רת קול תרועה

גרולו לנצח וי׃   לחם חנוחנום

נחצו׃   ׃׃ על מעורת   ׃צורר ׃

׃   ׃ווי לים

The War of the Sons of Light and the Sons of Darkness

CA. 100 B.C.E.-100 C.E.

"The War of the Sons of Light and the Sons of Darkness" appears to be the story of a war between the Jews (the "Sons of Light") and neighboring peoples such as the Moabites, Ammonites, Philistines, or possibly the Romans (the "Sons of Darkness" or "Hosts of Belial") who came to attack the Jews. The scroll predicts that at the "end of days" each side will win three times in turn, and then the "great hand of God" will win a victory for the "Sons of Light", who are the people of Israel. Whether the war was being waged at the time the scroll was written, or whether it was a prophecy of a future war, possibly at Judgment Day, is still not clear.

This remarkable scroll describes in detail the organization of the Jewish army (made up of soldiers chosen by the chief elders of the community) into fighting units of tens, fifties, hundreds, and thousands. It tells of the weapons they used—swords, spears, lances, javelins, shields—and of the banners they carried and the mottoes on them. Before the battle the Chief Priest exhorts the troops, and during the fighting itself the various companies are directed by the trumpet blasts of the priests for hurling stones and slinging javelins, for the march to attack, and withdrawal after the battle. There was a different kind of trumpet for each maneuver.

One of the Judean caves

A scroll

The Manual of Discipline

CA. 100 B.C.E.-100 C.E.

The scroll found in the cave at Ain Feshkha near the Dead Sea may offer clues to the identity of the original owners. It is the Manual of Discipline in which the aims of a Jewish sect are outlined, and is of great interest because of what it tells about the daily life of the people. The Manual discloses how new members were initiated into the sect, and the standards of conduct required of them. It describes the communal life and the sacramental meals in which they shared. The "volunteers," as the members were called, pledged themselves "to do what is good and right before God, as commanded by Moses and by all his servants the prophets." They undertook "to separate themselves from the society of wicked men; to love all the sons of light and to hate all the sons of darkness; to practice in community truth and modesty, to do righteously and justly, love mercy, and walk humbly in all their ways."

The Manual is very probably a document of the Essenes, who formed a group apart from the rest of the community. They did not believe in private property, but held all their belongings in common. They were celibate, wore only white garments, kept themselves scrupulously clean, and were most strict in observing the Sabbath. They believed in purification through immersion in water, and in the immortality of the soul. They hated untruthfulness, prohibited commerce since it might lead to cheating, and condemned slavery. Their living was made by agriculture and handicrafts. The Essene sect probably ceased to exist after the second century of the Common Era.

A scroll

Masada

(*Metsudah*)

73 C.E.

Masada (the word means fortress or stronghold) is a rugged cliff in the wilderness of Judea, about two and a half miles from the shore of the Dead Sea and not far from the Israeli town of En-Gedi. It is known as the Heroes' Rock in honor of the 960 besieged Zealots who made their last stand there during the Jewish rebellion against the Romans. Its fall in 73 C. E. marked the end of Jewish independence.

Access to Masada was originally difficult and dangerous, although in modern times a path along the southeastern incline has made it more accessible. The cliff is 440 feet high and has an area of about 20 acres. At its top are the remnants of a fortress hewn into the rock. There is a stone bench where guards once sat, barring the way to the summit. Dried date seeds have been found where they were dropped 1,900 years ago, along with fragments of ancient linen and leather, and of wood and metal from ancient weapons. Still standing is part of a wall that once surrounded a well. Stairs cut into the rock lead downward to deep holes used for collecting rainwater. There are even traces of ash and charred wood from long-dead fires.

Herod's Palace

During the war against Rome the Zealots occupied the fortress and used it as a base for surprise raids. When Jerusalem fell, the Zealots, led by Eleazar ben Yair, held out at Masada, defending it stubbornly for three years against ten thousand Roman soldiers of the Tenth Legion. The Romans camped at the foot of the cliff, hewed a path up its western side, and built a siege tower nearly 100 feet high, from which they catapulted stones and aimed their arrows into the fortress.

The defense of Masada was heroic, and its fall (there was no surrender) culminated in a supremely courageous act of martyrdom. When the attacking Romans reached the top of the cliff they found a dreadful solitude. Only two women and five children remained alive. The rest had burned down every building and killed themselves rather than surrender to the enemy. Their provisions were left intact to show it had not been want or hunger that had driven them to this step.

The memory of Masada is engraved on the hearts of Jews as an example and a rallying cry in their long struggle for freedom. The rock is now being explored by an archaeological team headed by Prof. Yigael Yadin.

Philo

FIRST CENTURY C.E.

Philo Judaeus, known in Hebrew as *Yediyah* (Beloved of God), was born at Alexandria about 10 B.C.E. He belonged to a family of great wealth and prestige and he dedicated his life to learning. He had a brother who was a favorite of Mark Antony and of the Roman nobility who then ruled Egypt. Alexandria, a center of Hellenistic culture, was second only to Jerusalem in the importance and size of its Jewish population. Philo came to be regarded as the greatest Jew born and bred in Egypt since Moses. Because his native city was steeped in Greek culture, Philo's command of Greek learning and philosophy was equaled by no other Jew; although he wrote in Greek, his message was Hebraic in content and spirit.

Ten volumes of his writings have survived; many others must have been lost. They represented Philo's lifelong teaching of the truths of Judaism and the Message of the Bible to the pagan world. He believed that the Children of Israel had been entrusted with the prophetic burden of being a "Light unto the Nations" and a "Servant of the Lord." He taught Scripture as the book of divine revelation and the source of the highest spiritual and moral values. To him the Mosaic Law fused the best of Hebraic and Greek teachings into one perfect whole. To synchronize the two cultures he developed an allegorical method of interpreting the Scriptures, to show that the literal narratives and precepts had an underlying philosophical and ethical meaning.

Philo is also remembered as the great champion of his people against the anti-Semitic attacks of Apion. In order to fan the hostility of the Egyptians against the Jews, Apion and his conspirators informed the demented Roman emperor Caligula that the Jews refused to worship him as a god, and would not permit his statue to be enshrined in their synagogues or in the Temple at Jerusalem. Philo was delegated to go to Rome to argue the case against Apion. He stood no chance with the mad emperor; but at just this time Caligula was assassinated. The new emperor was Claudius, a grandson of Mark Antony whose mother had been entrusted as a ward to Philo's brother by Mark Antony himself. The story of this episode is given in detail in Philo's book, *Against Apion*.

Although Philo's contemporary, Hillel, made a deep impression on Jewish life and thought, Philo himself was virtually ignored by his own people. This neglect may be accounted for by his having written in Greek, or by fear that he might wean the Greek-Jewish community from Hebraic learning. It may also have been due to the high esteem in which his writings were held by the Church. At any rate, it was not until some fifteen hundred years later that Philo was rediscovered and enshrined among the Jewish immortals.

ΝΟΜΩΝ ΙΕΡΩΝ ΑΛΛΗΓΟΡΙΑ
ΔΕΥΤΕΡΑ.

C v

Coins From the Second War of the Jews

(Bar Kokhba Revolt)

130-137 C..E.

When Emperor Hadrian paid a visit to Judea in the year 130 C.E., he was greeted with ceremony by the mixed population of the coastal cities, and coins were struck in his honor. They carry the inscription, *Adventus Augusti Judea,* and show Hadrian sacrificing at an altar while figures representing Judea and her children bring him gifts. The emperor was implored by the Jews to rebuild the Temple, which had lain in ruins since its destruction sixty years before. But Hadrian had other plans for Jerusalem. He intended to have the Temple rebuilt as a Roman shrine, with a statue of the emperor in what had once been the Holy of Holies.

Devout Jews, remembering that the destruction of the First Temple in 586 B.C.E. had been followed fifty years later by the return of the exiles to Judea under Cyrus, now hoped for another miraculous restoration.

When a young man of exceptional strength and beauty, a born leader, burst upon the scene, there were some who were ready to believe that he was the anointed one. To him Rabbi Akiba ben Joseph, greatest scholar and teacher of his day, is traditionally believed to have given the name of Bar Kokhba (Hebrew for Son of the Star), from the ancient prophecy recorded in the Book of Numbers: "There shall come a star out of Jacob, and a sceptre shall rise out of Israel."

By the time the revolt broke out in 132, Bar Kokhba's followers are said to have numbered in the hundreds of thousands. It is opined that in the space of a year these volunteers captured no fewer than 985 towns and villages throughout Samaria and Judea, in addition to Jerusalem. Bar Kokhba held Jerusalem long enough to set

up a revolutionary government. The discovery of coins has helped establish the date of the uprising. Close examination shows that they had been struck over medals originally issued in honor of Hadrian's visit to Judea, 130-131. Some of these reminted coins are dated "Year One of the Liberation of Israel," others "Year Two of the Liberation of Jerusalem"; still others mention no year, but read simply "For the Liberation of Jerusalem." Whether this is an indication that Bar Kokhba's rule over Jerusalem ended within three years is still not clear.

Other coins, valued at a shekel, depict a shrine and the scrolls of the Torah, presumably representing the Temple at Jerusalem. On the reverse are depicted the *lulav* and *ethrog,* the palm branch and citron used during the autumn festival of Sukkot. Some scholars have suggested that these may be an indication that the service of the Temple was restored during that festival in the year 132. This conjecture seems likely since other coins depict a jug, possibly representing the golden jug traditionally filled with water from the spring of Siloam and brought to the altar each day during the festival of Sukkot. Still others depict grapes, vine leaves, olive wreaths, and musical instruments, all possibly symbolic of the same harvest festival.

On some of the coins the faces of Roman emperors are still visible underneath the names with which they were overstruck. The first of these names, Shimon Nasi, refers to Bar Kokhba. The second is that of Eleazar, high priest, who may have been an uncle of Bar Kokhba, although this remains uncertain.

Until recent years, when new discoveries were made concerning Bar Kokhba by Professor Yadin at En-Gedi, on the western shores of the Dead Sea, these coins were the chief source of knowledge of the revolt.

Bar Kokhba Letters

132-135 C.E.

A packet of fifteen letters were found in 1960 in a cave of the desolate cliffs of En-Gedi, a few miles south of the frontier of Jordan on the western shore of the Dead Sea. Of these, nine are in Aramaic, four in Hebrew, and two in Greek. All had been sent by order of Bar Kokhba, although the signature in each instance seems that of a scribe rather than of the commander himself. From the transliteration of his name in one of the Greek letters, its pronunciation was definitely established for the first time. There is no longer any doubt that the exact name of Bar Kokhba was Shimon Bar Kosibah.

All but one of the letters are addressed to two subordinate commanders, Yehonatan (Jonathan) and Masabala. They are ordered to confiscate wheat belonging to a certain Tanhum Bar Yishmael; to take a certain Yeshua Bar Tadmoraya prisoner; and to punish the refractory population of Tekah, an agricultural town south of Bethlehem. Another letter orders the harvesting of the winter wheat in the area under the jurisdiction of the two commanders. One contains a reprimand: "You eat and drink of the property of the house of Israel, and care not for your brothers."

The final letter is addressed to "Yehuda Bar Menashe, at Kiryat Arabaya." It reads: "I have sent you two donkeys, so that you may send two men with them to Yehonatan and Masabala to load them with palm branches (*lulavim*) and *citrons* (*ethrogim*) and send them back to your camp. You, on your part, send others to bring you willows and myrtle . . . and send them to the camp."

In 1961 a packet containing more letters was found. One of these, which began, "On the 28th day of *Marheshvan,* year three of Shimon ben Kosibah, Prince of Israel," proved to be a contract leasing certain state lands in the name of "Yehonatan ben Mahanaim, administrator of Shimon ben Kosibah, Prince of Israel, in En-Gedi." Two similar deeds, likewise from En-Gedi, are dated just three days later. All three are written in Hebrew. The two other documents in the packet date from the first year of Bar Kokhba's rule, and are in Aramaic.

The story behind these documents is not yet complete. But as they—and possibly others, yet to be discovered—are deciphered, a significant episode in Jewish history begins to emerge from the obscurity of many hundreds of years. With the help of such documents, it may yet be possible to write a detailed history of Bar Kokhba's mysterious and sudden rise, and of the heroic revolt he led which ended so tragically.

The letters were discovered by an expedition sponsored by the Hebrew University and the Government of Israel and led by Yigael Yadin.

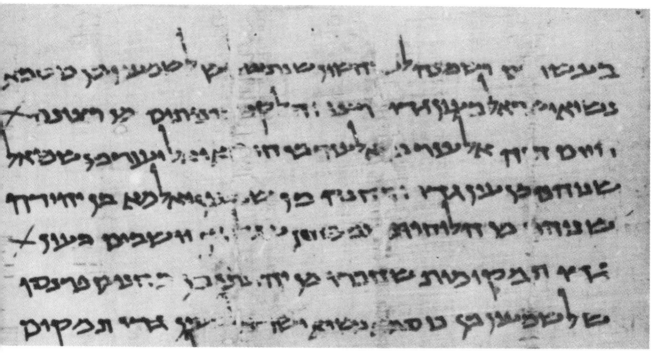

Packet of letters

The Shrine of Bar Yohai at Meron

135 C.E.

Mount Meron or Mount Jarmak, as it is called in Arabic, rises to an altitude of 3,962 feet and is the highest peak in Israel. On its slopes are the tombs of Rabbi Shimon bar Yohai and his son Eliezer.

On Lag B'Omer, Iyar 18, or twenty-eight days after Passover, Meron is the scene of an annual pilgrimage by tens of thousands of Israelis and visitors from all over the Jewish world. The tombs are alight with thousands of candles placed there in memory of loved ones, as a plea for the intercession of the saints to help the afflicted, or in thankfulness for God's mercy. Around huge bonfires in the courtyard and before the graves, the pilgrims dance and sing all through the night. In the morning many infant children are given their first haircut, and the shorn locks are thrown into the fire as an offering.

Shimon bar Yohai was a pupil of Rabbi Akiba, and a fierce antagonist of Rome. He was sentenced to death in the turbulent years of the Bar Kokhba rebellion. For thirteen years he and his son Eliezer hid themselves in a cave where, according to legend, a carob tree grew to feed them with its fruit and a spring welled forth to slake their thirst. To Bar Yohai was ascribed authorship of the mystic book of the Kabbalah, known as the *Zohar,* which abounds in hidden meanings, foretelling the triumph of good over evil and the ultimate coming of the Messiah.

The custom described above, known as *Hilula* (praise) of Shimon bar Yohai, was instituted in the sixteenth century by the kabbalists of Safed, a center of Jewish mysticism during the late Middle Ages, near Mount Meron; and from this city the assembled pilgrims gather to march to the shrine on Lag B'Omer.

Ark ornament

Menorah ornament

Engraved ossuary

Crypt with ornaments

Bet Shearim Catacombs

**SECOND-FOURTH
CENTURIES C.E.**

Cut into the soft limestone of Sheikh Abreiq, on the southern slope of Galilee above the Valley of Jezreel, are the catacombs of Bet Shearim, chief burial place for the Jews of Palestine and neighboring countries in the second century C. E.

The walls of the cemetery are decorated with geometric patterns and designs using human figures, animals, plants, fruits, and more. Specifically Jewish motifs include the menorah, lulav, ethrog, shofar, and oil jar. Also represented are the holy ark, Daniel in the lion's den, and Noah.

Inscriptions on the doors, walls, tombs, and slabs give the names of the persons buried there. These are in various alphabets—Greek, Hebrew, Latin, and Aramaic.

The town of Bet Shearim, frequently mentioned in the Talmud, was the residence of Judah ha-Nasi (Judah the Prince) and the meeting place of the Sanhedrin in the second half of the second century. Rabbi Judah's grave is among those in the Bet Shearim catacombs.

Professor Benjamin Mazar, Hebrew University Bible scholar and archaeologist who excavated the cemetery, has fixed the date of the destruction of Bet Shearim at 351 C. E.

Via Appia Catacombs

The Roman Jewish Catacombs

The Jewish community of Rome, dating back to the Hasmonean period (161 B.C.E.), is the oldest in Europe; and its catacombs are the oldest Jewish cemeteries in the western world. They had been forgotten for centuries until rediscovered in 1904. Of the several catacombs in various parts of Rome, the oldest are in Monteverde, Porta Portese, and Trastevere; others are in Via Appia Pignatelli, Via Appia Antica, Via Labicana, and Via Torlonia near Porta Pia.

Both Roman law and Jewish religious law forbade burial of the dead within city limits. Although the Romans cremated their dead, the Jews and early Christians buried them under the surface of the earth.

Carved, painted, or scratched on the tombs are crude pictures of e.g., menorah, lulav, ethrog, Torah scroll, a flask for oil or wine, shofar, and holy ark. Less fequent decorations are of birds, domestic animals, and trees. Occasionally there is a room with painted walls depicting classical and non-Jewish themes.

Entrance to Monteverde catacombs

59

Ancient Clay Lamps

A lamp is a simple, even a prosaic object—yet behind it lies a great advance, from the uncontrolled flickering of a torch to the steady illumination of a totally new epoch in human culture. It is no accident that the lamp is a symbol of faith and hope. For a lamp is far more than a utensil; it might almost be said to have a soul.

The earliest lamps were made of stone or clay, with a hollow at the center that contained the oil, and a "lip" at the rim to hold the burning wick. As the craft of pottery developed, the lip became a sort of nozzle. To increase the amount of light, an ingenious potter devised a lamp that held four wicks in four nozzles; such were the primitive Canannite lamps that have been unearthed in Palestine. A further development, introduced by the Israelites who settled in Canaan, was a lamp with a widened rim surrounding a deeper concavity. Still later lamps were placed on a raised pedestal, so that the light would extend still further.

Later, during the Babylonian exile, the Judeans met with lamps of a still different design—a smaller vessel, with the concavity half enclosed so as to protect the oil, and a closed nozzle that held the wick in place. Lamps of this sort were more easily carried from place to place without being extinguished. Despite these advantages, the Judeans appear not to have used such lamps on their return from Babylonia. Was it because they wished not to be reminded of the years of exile? At any rate, such lamps did eventually come into use in Judea.

Lamps such as have been described were all turned on a potter's wheel. During the Hellenistic era, however, beginning with the conquest of Palestine by Alexander the Great in 332 B.C.E., Judea first saw imported clay lamps that had been molded rather than turned. The clay was pressed into the two halves of a mold, an upper and a lower, which were allowed to dry and then joined by the process of firing. Here, once again, there appears to have been a conflict between old ways and new, with some who bitterly opposed the conquerors refusing to use the imported article. In tombs and ruins that have been excavated, lamps of all three types have been discovered —a mute witness to the struggle between ways of life, between rejection and accommodation.

The Roman conquerors of Palestine brought with them an improved lamp, whose closed top had two openings, the smaller for filling the vessel with oil, the larger to hold the wick, and provided with handles to make carrying easier. Often such lamps were very large, with several wicks and elaborate decoration. Roman lamps, for example, showed likenesses of gods and emperors, or scenes of games and races or gladiatorial contests. The Jews, adapting such designs to their own purposes, adorned them with scriptural or symbolic designs. Similarly, during the first and second centuries of the current era, lamps made by Christians were decorated with such symbols as the fish and the dove. Around the same time, inscriptions first began to be used alike by Christians, Moslems and Jews. Pictured here are lamps containing Jewish motifs. One depicts Samson in the act of toppling the temple of the Philistines (Judges 16:29-30); another shows Daniel in the den of lions (Daniel 6:17); a third, the spies returning from Canaan with clusters of grapes (Numbers 13:23). A fourth lamp, this one made of bronze, and designed to resemble a menorah, shows a lulav and ethrog (palm branch and citrus) on one side, and a shofar on the other. This lamp is unique, and is in a valuable collection owned by Miriam Schaar Schloessinger of New York City.

Menorah, lulav, shofar

Daniel

Spies

Samson

Capernaum Synagogue

SECOND-THIRD CENTURY C.E.

Capernaum is a name well known to Christians because it was there that Jesus began his mission after leaving Nazareth. In the first chapters of the Gospel of Mark we are told that Jesus and his disciples went into Capernaum, "and straightway on the Sabbath day he entered into the synagogue, and taught." Capernaum, situated at the northern edge of the Sea of Galilee, was originally called Kfar Nahum, "the village of Nahum." The present name is derived from the Greek spelling of the two words.

The remains of the synagogue are in a good state of preservation, and give an idea of the typical synagogue in the Palestine of the second or third century. Apparently built upon the ruins of an earlier century, it contained many carved lintels and friezes, sculptured capitals, and elaborately decorated arches. The rectangular hall was divided by columns into a nave and three aisles. The Holy Ark was placed against the south wall, to face Jerusalem. The motifs used in the carving, like those in other buildings of the same period, consist chiefly of palm trees, grape clusters, the seven-branched candelabrum (menorah), and the ram's horn (shofar). The floor was covered with large slabs of stone. Against the dark basalt of the region, the sight of the two-story structure of white marble rising on the shores of the Sea of Galilee must have been impressive indeed.

Shield of David   *Lulav*   *Menorah*

Dura-Europos' Synagogue Murals

THIRD CENTURY C.E.

The earliest known synagogue with mural decoration containing human figures is the ancient synagogue of Dura-Europos. The thirty panels that have been preserved (about half of the original decorations) illustrate episodes from the Bible. Among the figures are the patriarchs, Abraham, Isaac and Jacob; the twelve sons of Jacob; the two sons of Joseph; Moses, Aaron, and Miriam; the prophets Samuel, Elijah, and Ezekiel; Kings Saul, David, and Solomon; and the characters of the Purim story, Esther, Ahasuerus, Mordecai, and Haman.

Until the discovery of this synagogue, the art of the Hellenistic Jewish period was known only from the Roman catacombs. The find at Dura-Europos is significant proof that in the third century a Jewish community had permitted the drawing of human figures in the sanctuary, a practice proscribed in the Second Commandment: "Thou shalt not make a graven image."

The murals furnish an insight into the inner life, the hopes and aspirations of a distant, small Jewish community in the early years

Valley of dry bones (Ezekiel, VI)

of the dispersion. They show how a third century Jewish group believed biblical personalities looked, and illustrates the accommodation and synthesis of the Greek and Jewish world in the early centuries of the Christian era.

Dura-Europos lay between Damascus and Baghdad, on the right bank of the Euphrates. The synagogue built in its ancient city wall was one of the earliest before the Common Era. In 256 C.E. the city was besieged by the Sassanians (a Persian dynasty), and in order to fortify it the occupying Romans enclosed some of the buildings, close to the city wall, in a mud brick embankment, much like those built today as protection against flood waters. Fortunately the synagogue (and incidentally the Christian community house as well) was in the area thus bricked up. In 1932-33, an expedition from Yale University and a French archaeological academy excavated the site and came upon the synagogue.

The site of Dura-Europos itself was discovered in 1921 by the archaeologist James Henry Breasted, and was excavated by a Yale University expedition under the direction of M. Rostovtzeff, whose report in several volumes was published between 1929 and 1956.

The Dura synagogue murals are the prize exhibits today at the National Museum in Damascus, Syria.

Consecration of Tabernacle and Priests

After the first dig

Relief adorning chapel showing menorah, lulav, etrog, shofar

View from the West

The chapel

The Synagogue of Ostia, Port of Ancient Rome

FOURTH CENTURY

The summer resort of Ostia, at the mouth of the Tiber River, was in ancient times the port city of Rome, at which ships bringing goods to the capital discharged their cargoes. In 1961, a construction crew at work improving the highway from Rome to the port dug up the remains of a fourth century synagogue, a discovery of great historical importance.

Originally the building stood on the waterfront of the ancient city. Of its several parts, the earliest appear to have been constructed about the end of the first century, with additions and changes culminating in a partial reconstruction during the fourth century. The main entrance was from the Via Severina, a road parallel to the shore. From it one passed into a narrow vestibule, on one side of which were a series of small rooms, and on the other the prayer hall and a room containing an oven where *matzah,* or unleavened bread, presumably was baked. The latter room also contained a marble-topped table which no doubt was used for kneading dough, and a row of large earthenware vats used for storing wine, oil, and other comestibles.

The prayer hall, a large rectangular room whose back wall is slightly curved, faced east-southeast, in the direction of Jerusalem. In front it was divided into three sections by a low wall. The roof was supported by columns of gray marble, with white marble bases and capitals; and the floor was paved partly with black and white mosaic, partly with colored marble laid in geometric designs. A unique feature of the building, unlike anything previously discovered, was a brickwork shrine, approached by steps, with a pair of columns in front in which the Holy Ark was kept. An architrave supported by the columns had carved within it the *menorah, lulav, ethrog,* and *shofar.* Another feature is a sunken rectangular basin which may have been used as a ritual bath.

The excavations, carried out under direction of Professor Maria Floriani Squarciapino, is the first proof of the existence of a Jewish community in ancient Ostia.

ΑΥΤΗΗΓΕΝΕΑΖΗΤΟΥΝΤΩΝΑΥΤΟΝ
ΖΗΤΟΥΝΤΩΝΤΟΠΡΟCΩΠΟΝΤΟΥ
ΙΑΚΩΒ
ΔΙΑΨΑΛΜΑ
ΑΡΑΤΕΠΥΛΑCΟΙΑΡΧΟΝΤΕCΥΜΩΝ
ΚΑΙΕΠΑΡΘΗΤΕΠΥΛΑΙΑΙΩΝΙΟΙ
ΚΑΙΕΙCΕΛΕΥCΕΤΑΙΟΒΑCΙΛΕΥCΤΗCΔΟ...
ΤΙCΕCΤΙΝΟΥΤΟCΟΒΑCΙΛΕΥCΤΗCΔΟ...
ΚΕΚΡΑΤΑΙΟCΚΑΙΔΥΝΑΤΟC
ΚΕΔΥΝΑΤΟCΕΝΠΟΛΕΜΩ
ΑΡΑΤΕΠΥΛΑCΟΙΑΡΧΟΝΤΕCΥΜΩΝ
ΚΑΙΕΠΑΡΘΗΤΕΠΥΛΑΙΑΙΩΝΙΟΙ
ΚΑΙΕΙCΕΛΕΥCΕΤΑΙΟΒΑCΙΛΕΥCΤΗCΔ...
ΚΕΤΩΝΔΥΝΑΜΕΩΝΑΥΤΟCΕCΤΙΝΟΥ
ΤΟCΟΒΑCΙΛΕΥCΤΗCΔΟΞΗC
ΨΑΛΜΟCΤΩΔΑΔ
ΚΑΙΠΡΟCCΕΚΕΚΡΑΤΗΝΨΥΧΗΝΜΟΥ
ΕΠΙCΟΙΠΕΠΟΙΘΑΜΗΚΑΤΑΙCΧΥΝΟ...
ΜΗΔΕΚΑΤΑΓΕΛΑCΑΤΩCΑΝΜΟΥΟΙ
ΕΧΘΡΟΙΜΟΥ
ΚΑΙΓΑΡΠΑΝΤΕCΟΙΥΠΟΜΕΝΟΝΤΕCCΕ
ΟΥΜΗΚΑΤΑΙCΧΥΝΘΩCΙΝ
ΑΙCΧΥΝΘΗΤΩCΑΝΟΙΑΝΟΜΟΥΝΤΕC
ΔΙΑΚΕΝΗC
ΤΑCΟΔΟΥCCΟΥΚΕΓΝΩΡΙCΟΝΜΟΙ
ΚΑΙΤΑCΤΡΙΒΟΥCCΟΥΔΙΔΑΞΟΝΜΕ
ΟΔΗΓΗCΟΝΜΕΕΠΙΤΗΝΑΛΗΘΕΙΑCΟΥ
ΚΑΙΔΙΔΑΞΟΝΜΕΟΤΙCΥΕΙΟΘCΟCΩΡΜ...
ΚΑΙCΕΥΠΕΜΕΙΝΑΟΛΗΝΤΗΝΗΜΕΡΑΝ
ΜΝΗCΘΗΤΙΤΩΝΟΙΚΤΕΙΡΜΩΝCΟΥΚΕ
ΚΑΙΤΑΕΛΕΗCΟΥΟΤΙΑΠΟΤΟΥΑΙΩΝΟ...
ΑΜΑΡΤΙΑCΝΕΟΤΗΤΟCΜΟΥΚΑΙΑΓΝΟΙΑ...
ΓΝΟΙΑCΜΗΜΝΗCΘΗC
ΚΑΤΑΤΟΕΛΕΟCCΟΥΜΝΗCΘΗΤΙΜΟΥCΥ
ΕΝΕΚΑΤΗCΧΡΗCΤΟΤΗΤΟCCΟΥΚΕ
ΧΡΗCΤΟCΚΑΙΕΥΘΥCΟΚC
ΔΙΑΤΟΥΤΟΝΟΜΟΘΕΤΗCΕΙΑΜΑΡΤΑ...
ΝΟΝΤΑCΕΝΟΔΩ
ΟΔΗΓΗCΕΙΠΡΑΕΙCΕΝΚΡΙCΕΙ
ΔΙΔΑΞΕΙΠΡΑΕΙCΟΔΟΥCΑΥΤΟΥ
ΠΑCΑΙΑΙΟΔΟΙΚΥΕΛΕΟCΚΑΙΑΛΗΘΕΙΑ
ΤΟΙCΕΚΖΗΤΟΥCΙΝΤΗΝΔΙΑΘΗΚΗΝΑΥ
ΤΟΥΚΑΙΤΑΜΑΡΤΥΡΙΑΑΥΤΟΥ
ΕΝΕΚΑΤΟΥΟΝΟΜΑΤΟCCΟΥΚΕ
ΚΑΙΕΙΛΑCΘΗΤΗΑΜΑΡΤΙΑΜΟΥΠΟΛΛΗ
ΓΑΡΕCΤΙΝ
ΤΙCΕCΤΙΝΑΝΘΟCΟΦΟΒΟΥΜΕΝΟCΤΝΚΝ

ΝΟΜΟΘΕΤΗCΕΙΑΥΤΩΕΝΟΔΩΗΗΡΕΤ...
ΗΨΥΧΗΑΥΤΟΥΕΝΑΓΑΘΟΙCΑΥΛΙCΘΗC...
ΚΑΙΤΟCΠΕΡΜΑΑΥΤΟΥΚΛΗΡΟΝΟΜΗ...
ΚΡΑΤΑΙΩΜΑΚCΤΩΝΦΟΒΟΥΜΕΝΩΝΧ...
ΚΑΙΗΔΙΑΘΗΚΗΑΥΤΟΥΤΟΥΔΗΛΩCΑ...
ΟΙΟΦΘΑΛΜΟΙΜΟΥΔΙΑΠΑΝΤΟCΠΡ...
ΟΤΙΑΥΤΟCΕΚCΠΑCΕΙΕΚΠΑΓΙΔΟCΤΟΥC
ΠΟΔΑCΜΟΥ
ΕΠΙΒΛΕΨΟΝΕΠΕΜΕΚΑΙΕΛΕΗCΟΝΜΕ
ΟΤΙΜΟΝΟΓΕΝΗCΚΑΙΠΤΩΧΟCΕΙΜΙΕ...
ΑΙΘΛΙΨΕΙCΤΗCΚΑΡΔΙΑCΜΟΥΕΠΛΗ
ΘΥΝΘΗCΑΝ
ΕΚΤΩΝΑΝΑΓΚΩΝΜΟΥΕΞΑΓΑΓΕΜΕ
ΙΔΕΤΗΝΤΑΠΕΙΝΩCΙΝΜΟΥΚΑΙΤΟΝΚ...
ΚΑΙΑΦΕCΠΑCΑCΤΑCΑΜΑΡΤΙΑCΜΟΥ
ΙΔΕΤΟΥCΕΧΘΡΟΥCΜΟΥΟΤΙΕΠΛΗ...
ΚΑΙΜΕΙCΟCΑΔΙΚΟΝΕΜΕΙCΗCΑΝΜΕ
ΦΥΛΑΞΟΝΤΗΝΨΥΧΗΝΜΟΥΚΑΙΡΥCΑΙ...
ΜΗΚΑΤΑΙCΧΥΝΘΕΙΗΝΟΤΙΗΛΠΙCΑ...
ΑΚΑΚΟΙΚΑΙΕΥΘΕΙCΕΚΟΛΛΩΝΤΟΜΟΙ
ΟΤΙΥΠΕΜΕΙΝΑCΕ
ΛΥΤΡΩCΑΙΟΘCΤΟΝΙΛΕΚΠΑCΩΝΤΩΝ
ΘΛΙΨΕΩΝΑΥΤΟΥ
ΤΟΥΔΑΔ

ΚΡΙΝΟΝΜΕΚΕΟΤΙΕΓΩΕΝΑΚΑΚΙΑ
ΜΟΥΕΠΟΡΕΥΘΗΝ
ΚΑΙΕΠΙΤΩΚΩΕΛΠΙΖΩΝΟΥΜΗΑCΘΕΝ...
ΤΗCΩCΟΝΤΟΥCΕΝΕΦΡΟΥCΕΜΟΥΚΑΙ
ΤΗΝΚΑΡΔΙΑΝΜΟΥ
ΟΤΙΤΟΕΛΕΟCCΟΥΚΑΤΕΝΑΝΤΙΤΩΝΟ
ΦΘΑΛΜΩΝΜΟΥΕCΤΙΝ
ΚΑΙΕΥΗΡΕCΤΗCΑΕΝΤΗΑΛΗΘΕΙΑCΟΥ
ΟΥΚΕΚΑΘΙCΑΜΕΤΑCΥΝΕΔΡΙΟΥΜΑΤΑ...
ΚΑΙΜΕΤΑΠΑΡΑΝΟΜΟΥΝΤΩΝΟΥΜΗ
ΕΙCΕΛΘΩ
ΕΜΕΙCΗCΑΕΚΚΛΗCΙΑΝΠΟΝΗΡΕΥ...
ΚΑΙΜΕΤΑΑCΕΒΩΝΟΥΜΗΚΑΘΙCΩ
ΝΙΨΟΜΑΙΕΝΑΘΩΟΙCΤΑCΧΕΙΡΑCΜΟΥ
ΚΑΙΚΥΚΛΩCΩΤΟΘΥCΙΑCΤΗΡΙΟΝCΟΥΚΕ
ΤΟΥΑΚΟΥCΑΙΦΩΝΗΝΑΙΝΕCΕΩC
ΚΑΙΔΙΗΓΗCΑCΘΑΙΠΑΝΤΑΤΑΘΑΥΜΑCΙΑ...
ΚΕΗΓΑΠΗCΑΕΥΠΡΕΠΙΑΝΟΙΚΟΥCΟΥ
ΚΑΙΤΟΠΟΝCΚΗΝΩΜΑΤΟCΔΟΞΗCCΟΥ
ΜΗCΥΝΑΠΟΛΕCΗCΜΕΤΑΑCΕΒΩΝΤΗΝ
ΨΥΧΗΝΜΟΥ
ΚΑΙΜΕΤΑΑΝΔΡΩΝΑΙΜΑΤΩΝΤΗΝ...ΗΝΜ...
ΩΝΕΝΧΕΡCΙΝΑΝΟΜΙΑ
ΗΔΕΞΙΑΑΥΤΩΝΕΠΛΗCΘΗΔΩΡΩΝ

ΕΓΩΔΕΕΝΑΚΑΚΙΑCΟΥΜΕΙCΕΚΑΙCΚΗΡΕΟCΜΕ

Codex Sinaiticus

FOURTH CENTURY

The Codex Sinaiticus is a Greek translation of the Bible dating from the fourth century of the current era. It contains parts of Genesis, Numbers, Chronicles, Ezra, Nehemiah, Isaiah, Jeremiah, the Minor Prophets, Psalms, Proverbs, Ecclesiastes, Job, Song of Songs, Esther, and books of the Apocrypha, in addition to a complete text of the New Testament.

The Codex is named after the monastery of St. Catherine on Mt. Sinai, where it was found in 1844. It was rescued from burning by Constantine von Tischendorf, a German Bible scholar, whose dogged efforts to preserve the manuscript and to deposit it in the Imperial Library at St. Petersburg make a tale of adventure and intrigue as romantic as any fiction.

In 1933 the Union of Soviet Socialist Republics sold the Codex for £100,000 (then nearly half a million dollars) raised by popular subscription in England through the British Museum, where it is now a treasured possession.

The Codex is written on vellum, four columns to the page. Evidently it is the work of three scribes, two of whom were inexperienced and deficient in spelling.

Zodiac floor

Bet Alpha Synagogue Floor Mosaic

SIXTH CENTURY

In 1928, farmers digging an irrigation ditch below Mount Gilboa in the Valley of Jezreel uncovered a mosaic floor. Later excavations under the direction of Professor Sukenik of the Hebrew University showed it to be virtually intact—the most complete so far discovered in Israel. Now on display at Kibbutz Hepzibah, it is called by the name of its sister kibbutz nearby, because the original synagogue was known as Bet Alpha. Built in the sixth century C.E., the synagogue consisted of three sections: a rectangular court, a narrow hall, and beyond the hall the prayer room or synagogue proper. Here the Holy Ark was kept in a niche in the southern wall, which faced Jerusalem.

The main feature of the mosaic floor shows Phoebus, the sun, in a horse-drawn chariot, within a circle depicting the signs of the Zodiac. At each corner is a winged female figure symbolizing one of the four seasons. The whole may be intended to represent God's rule of the universe. The mosaic also includes a scene of the sacrifice of Isaac, with the boy and his father at the right, the hand of God and the ram in the center, and two servants waiting with a donkey at the left. Above the ram are the words from Genesis, "And behold a ram." Over a branch symbolizing the thicket are the first two words of a verse in Genesis XXII:12: "Lay not your hand upon the boy! For now I know that you fear God, seeing that you have not withheld your son, even your only son." Abraham's obedience in agreeing to sacrifice Isaac, and the appearance of the ram caught in the thicket, are portrayed as symbolic confirmation of God's covenant with Israel. The whole has a naive, childlike charm.

Sacrifice of Isaac

The Siddur of Rabbi Amram

870

Rabbi Amram ben Sheshna was head of the Academy at Sura, Babylonia, between the years 858 and 870, and the author of more than two hundred responsa (written decisions by rabbis on questions of Jewish law) that have come down to us. The most famous of these, a *teshuvah* (responsum) sent to Barcelona, Spain, in 870, has immortalized him in Jewish history since it established the complete order of the liturgy. The siddur we use today, although edited and considerably changed, still carries the name of Rabbi Amram. This was the first time that the regulations, order, and sequence of the siddur were written down completely. To accompany it Rabbi Amram wrote a running commentary.

The rabbis and scholars watched carefully to see that no deviations were made by the precentor from traditional Judaism, and that no doctrine from Christianity or any religious idea foreign to Judaism, or any improper and indecent statements, were insinuated into the service.

Despite the wide dispersion of the Jewish people over the world, there was little significant variance among the liturgies of Babylonia, Palestine, and the Mediterranean countries. But as the Dispersion continued to expand there was a growing fear of disunity; and indeed there were grounds for such a fear. From the days of the Gaon Yehudai (760-764 C. E.), a spate of questions were addressed to the Babylonian academies about the liturgy, the weekly Torah reading, and other points of law related to the synagogue and the service. To answer the need, the geonim wrote the responsa which were later incorporated into the tradition. It remained for Rabbi Amram to set down the content, order, customs, and legal regulations of the prayers for weekdays, festivals, holidays, and fast days, including the order of the Haggadah service for Passover. His authorities were the Babylonian and the Jerusalem Talmuds, and the responsa of Rabbis Yehudai and Natrunai and the other geonim of Sura. In addition he based his siddur on the practices established in the academies of Pumbeditha and Sura.

Rabbi Amram's siddur influenced the liturgy and ritual of Spain, Portugal, and the Mediterranean lands. Although used widely, however, it was not canonized. Perhaps because of its very popularity it was also supplemented, changed, amended, and emended as few books have been. This is evident from the three manuscript copies that have come down to us. The arrangement of the prayer books used today, the siddur and mahzor, nevertheless dates from Rabbi Amram, who compiled them and gave them the stamp of his authority.

כדור רב עמרם ז"ל

אקרויפא, וישחד מפניהם אבות...

לשאת על עסקי אליים ויקבלו...

קוריאן מין תחילה בלא תורה נשוא...

תורה ומכתב ויחתנו לישראל הארץ ו...

ויעמדו מעשיהם וייצאו עמם תמיד בל...

דאם אחד רק בברי תמילה נסמכן ומיך...

שומרים אות השסך ולא היה מלך בארץ קד...

אשר היה עשרה במלחמה נ עתנת שמוח...

יגבא עד פעם שיטאו עמהם היהודים במ...

פעם יאוחז חיים גבר יהודי אחד בחרב וחבריח אר...

הערים גבאים על קד ושמוהן עליהם אשר קוד לפור...

יעבא במשפטם הראשון ויהן בדברים גולה ויפתביס...

עד אימר והג יל וייעמד את ל השר לשוב במ...

כי הכוח ועשתע סרח כו...ה ותעמדהו ל... וגם הוא...

נאות כי גהנול היד גם אבי הגשמה איש יבזק כר...

הבוא הריהו ודרך החיים ...נו כפתמייו מלכי מקד...

ומלכי ירב את הדברים האלה חרה להם מאד ויפלאו...

שלח... אל שרי קזריא דברי צידופים עליפוריל לאמר...

מנעכם לשוב באמונת היהודים שהם כעובדים ותחת...

ורי כל זומות וידברו דבריים שאין לנ ספר ויטון את...

לב השרים לרע ויאמר השר הגדול ויהודי מהלנו...

להרבות דברים יבואן מחכמי ישראל ומחכמי יון...

ומחכמי ערב וגידרו לפנינו ולפנים כל אחד מהם...

Khazar Document

CA. 950

In the dark ancient chamber of the Cairo Genizah, Solomon Schechter discovered a document, written about the middle of the tenth century C. E., which sheds light on a romantic period in Jewish history. It dates back to the time when Hasdai ibn Shaprut, prime minister of the Caliphs of Cordova, a scholar and outstanding Jewish leader, corresponded with Joseph, King of the Jewish Khazars.

Khazaria, a powerful Jewish kingdom, lay at the eastern extreme of the then known European world, between the Caucasian Mountains and the Caspian Sea, and between the Volga and Dnieper Rivers. As Chief Minister of Foreign and Commercial Affairs, Hasdai received merchants, guests, emissaries, and ambassadors. One day he heard by chance of the existence of Khazaria from some Byzantine messengers. Believing that the Khazars were the Ten Lost Tribes of Israel, Hasdai did not rest. He wrote a long letter to King Joseph in which he described the people and the country in which he lived, his position with the Caliph of Cordova, and his deep interest in his Jewish brethren the world over. King Joseph replied with an account of how the Khazars had come to adopt the Jewish religion.

Hasdai's excitement may have abated when he learned from the king that the Khazars were originally a group of heathen tribes who had adopted Judaism, and not part of the alleged Ten Lost Tribes at all. Hasdai probably never did avail himself of King Joseph's invitation to visit Khazaria.

The Genizah Khazar document consists of one quire of two leaves or four pages measuring 7¾″ by 5⅜″. Beautifully written in square Hebrew cursive characters, it consists of about a hundred lines altogether. The language is biblical Hebrew, with occasional rabbinical phrases. It is a fragment of a letter written by an unnamed Khazar Jew to another unnamed person, addressed as "my lord," who may have been Hasdai himself.

The document is in the Genizah collection at Cambridge University, England.

ליהוֹית רבני רתיכא נאפך עמא לקרוזי׃
ויפשע אדום מתחת יד יהודה עד היום
הזה אז תפשע לבנה בעת ההיא׃ ומלדן
אירומאי מתחות יד אינש יהודה עד יומא
הדין בכין מרדו יתבי ולבנה בעידנא ההוא׃
ויתר דברי יורם וכל אשר עשה הלוא הם
כתובים על ספר דברי הימים למלכי יהודה׃
ושאר פתגמי יורם וכל דעבד הלא אינון
כתיבין על ספר פתגמי יומיא למלכא דבית
יהודה׃ וישכב יורם עם אבתו ויקבר עם
אבתו בעיר דוד וימלך אחזיהו בנו תחתו׃
ושכיב יורם עם אבהתוהי ואתקבר עם
אבהתוהי בקרתא דדוד ומלך אחזיה
בריה תחותוהי׃ בשנת שתים
עשרה שנה ליורם בן אחאב מלך ישראל
מלך אחזיהו בן יורם מלך יהודה׃ בשנת
תרתא עסרי שנין ליורם בר אחאב מלכא
דישראל מלך אחזיה בר יורם מלך שבטא
דבית יהודה׃ בן עשרים ושתים שנה
אחזיהו במלכו ושנה אחת מלך בירושלם
ושם אמו עתליהו בת עמרי מלך ישראל׃
בר עסרין ותרתין שנין אחזיה כד מלך
ושתא חדא מלך בירוש ושום אמיה עתליה
בת עמרי מלכא דישראל וילך בדרך בית
אחאב ויעש הרע בעיני יהוה כבית אחאב
כי חתנ... אחא... זל בארח בית

The Hebrew Vowel System

Hebrew is a language made up of consonants. Unlike English, Hebrew words all begin with consonants; and all rootwords are consonants, usually three letters.

The Torah scroll, which is read in the synagogue on Sabbaths and holidays, and on Monday and Thursday mornings, contains no vocalization. As the Jews were more and more widely dispersed and Hebrew ceased to be their spoken language, it became difficult to study the Holy Scriptures without some aid in pronunciation. Words could be pronounced in many different ways, and as a result, the text of the Scriptures could be misconstrued and mistranslated. Accordingly, vowel aids of various sorts came into being.

The vowel points found in Hebrew books today were developed by the scholars of Tiberias in Palestine, about the tenth century. These points are written below or within the line.

In Babylonia at this time, the vowel system was written above the line, as shown on the accompanying page. This system, however, was not accepted. The fragment illustrated was discovered in the Cairo Genizah.

Tiberian vowel system (Spanish Bible, 1479), Exodus, Ch. 8

שירת האזינו (דברים לב, לג–מג)

וְרֹאשׁ פְּתָנִים אַכְזָר · חֲלֹא הוּא כָּמֻס עִמָּדִי
חָתֻם בְּאֹצְרֹתָי · לִי נָקָם וְשִׁלֵּם
לְעֵת תָּמוּט רַגְלָם · מִקָּרוֹב יוֹם אֵידָם
וְחָשׁ עֲתִדֹת לָמוֹ · כִּי יָדִין יְהוָה עַמּוֹ
וְעַל עֲבָדָיו יִתְנֶחָם · כִּי יִרְאֶה כִּי אָזְלַת יָד
וְאֶפֶס עָצוּר וְעָזוּב · וְאָמַר אֵי אֱלֹהֵימוֹ
צוּר חָסָיוּ בוֹ · אֲשֶׁר חֵלֶב זְבָחֵימוֹ יֹאכֵלוּ
יִשְׁתּוּ יֵין נְסִיכָם · יָקוּמוּ וְיַעְזְרֻכֶם
יְהִי עֲלֵיכֶם סִתְרָה · רְאוּ עַתָּה כִּי אֲנִי אֲנִי הוּא
וְאֵין אֱלֹהִים עִמָּדִי · אֲנִי אָמִית וַאֲחַיֶּה
מָחַצְתִּי וַאֲנִי אֶרְפָּא · וְאֵין מִיָּדִי מַצִּיל
כִּי אֶשָּׂא אֶל שָׁמַיִם יָדִי · וְאָמַרְתִּי חַי אָנֹכִי לְעֹלָם
אִם שַׁנּוֹתִי בְּרַק חַרְבִּי · וְתֹאחֵז בְּמִשְׁפָּט יָדִי
אָשִׁיב נָקָם לְצָרָי · וְלִמְשַׂנְאַי אֲשַׁלֵּם
אַשְׁכִּיר חִצַּי מִדָּם · וְחַרְבִּי תֹּאכַל בָּשָׂר
מִדַּם חָלָל וְשִׁבְיָה · מֵרֹאשׁ פַּרְעוֹת אוֹיֵב
הַרְנִינוּ גוֹיִם עַמּוֹ · כִּי דַם עֲבָדָיו יִקּוֹם
וְנָקָם יָשִׁיב לְצָרָיו · וְכִפֶּר אַדְמָתוֹ עַמּוֹ

וַיָּבֹא מֹשֶׁה וַיְדַבֵּר אֶת כָּל דִּבְרֵי הַשִּׁירָה הַזֹּאת בְּאָזְנֵי הָעָם הוּא וְהוֹשֵׁעַ בִּן נוּן ‧ וַיְכַל מֹשֶׁה לְדַבֵּר אֶת כָּל הַדְּבָרִים הָאֵלֶּה אֶל כָּל יִשְׂרָאֵל ‧ וַיֹּאמֶר אֲלֵהֶם שִׂימוּ לְבַבְכֶם לְכָל הַדְּבָרִים אֲשֶׁר אָנֹכִי מֵעִיד בָּכֶם הַיּוֹם אֲשֶׁר תְּצַוֻּם אֶת בְּנֵיכֶם לִשְׁמֹר לַעֲשׂוֹת אֶת כָּל דִּבְרֵי הַתּוֹרָה הַזֹּאת ‧ כִּי לֹא דָבָר רֵק הוּא מִכֶּם כִּי הוּא חַיֵּיכֶם וּבַדָּבָר הַזֶּה תַּאֲרִיכוּ יָמִים עַל הָאֲדָמָה אֲשֶׁר אַתֶּם עֹבְרִים אֶת הַיַּרְדֵּן שָׁמָּה לְרִשְׁתָּהּ ‧

וַיְדַבֵּר יְהוָה אֶל מֹשֶׁה בְּעֶצֶם הַיּוֹם הַזֶּה לֵאמֹר ‧ עֲלֵה אֶל הַר הָעֲבָרִים הַזֶּה הַר נְבוֹ אֲשֶׁר בְּאֶרֶץ מוֹאָב אֲשֶׁר עַל פְּנֵי יְרֵחוֹ וּרְאֵה אֶת אֶרֶץ כְּנַעַן אֲשֶׁר אֲנִי נֹתֵן לִבְנֵי יִשְׂרָאֵל לַאֲחֻזָּה ‧ וּמֻת בָּהָר אֲשֶׁר אַתָּה עֹלֶה שָׁמָּה וְהֵאָסֵף אֶל עַמֶּיךָ כַּאֲשֶׁר מֵת אַהֲרֹן אָחִיךָ בְּהֹר הָהָר וַיֵּאָסֶף אֶל עַמָּיו ‧

Ben Asher or Aleppo Codex

TENTH CENTURY

Three hundred miles north of Jerusalem, in the rocky hills of Syria, lies Aleppo, one of the oldest Jewish communities in the world (now almost extinct). During the Middle Ages it was known as a center of Jewish learning. For more than five centuries the oldest of its ancient synagogues, the Mustaribah, was the repository of the *Keter Torah* (Crown of the Torah) or Aleppo Codex, one of the oldest existing complete texts of the Bible, with vocalization and notes for cantillation.

In 1947, after the decision of the United Nations to make Israel an independent state, vicious riots occurred in Aleppo, as in many other cities in the Middle East. Jews were killed, houses were looted, and synagogues were desecrated and destroyed. The Jewish world was appalled to learn that the Mustaribah, home of the famous *Keter Torah,* had been burned. For years afterward there seemed little hope that the priceless book would be seen again. Happily, it had been saved by a miracle; and in October, 1960, it was delivered into the hands of the late Ben-Zvi, then president of Israel.

The Aleppo Codex contains the text from the school of Rabbi Aaron ben Moshe ben Asher, greatest and most renowned of the Tiberian Masoretes. These were scholars who devoted themselves to a minute study and memorization of the Bible text so as to transmit it intact from generation to generation. Rabbi ben Asher lived in the first half of the tenth century, and it is on his text that Luther's translation of the Bible into German and the King James translation into English are based.

Originally the codex consisted of 380 parchment leaves (or 760 pages), measuring ten by thirteen inches, and mainly written in three columns. It now contains 294 pages; the rest, about one-fourth, were burned in 1948.

EP

מורה נבוכים

עם פירוש. שם טוב ועם פירוש האפודי

ושער אחד יודיע בוכוונת כל פרק מפרקי המורה

ושער יכלול בו כל המלות זרות שבאו בו והועיל למעיינים בו
כאשר כתב בהקדמת השער

גם סדור כל פסוקי התורה והנביאים אשר באו זכרם
בכלל המאמר הזה

למען יהיה כשלחן ערוך לאשר נגע אלהים
בלבו להנות כמורה צדק הזה

כדפם באמצעות הסר מאכזיפיקו מיסיר אלוויזי בראגדין בן האדון מאכזיפיקו מיסיר פירו בראגדין:

שנת חמשת אלפים ושלש מאות ואחד עשר לבריאת עולם כמנה רביעית לאחכלים
קדאבוס פראנצ'יסקו דנוס ירס יאון

בוינציאה

Maimonides' "Guide to the Perplexed"

1190

Moses ben Maimon, popularly known as Rambam or Maimonides, was the greatest Jewish scholar, philosopher, and scientist of the Middle Ages. His name is coupled with that of the Lawgiver for whom he was named, in the wellknown epigram, "From Moses to Moses there was none like unto Moses." His works and personality influenced both Christian and Moslem thinking in the fields of medicine, religion, philosophy, and jurisprudence. He was born in Cordova in 1135, scion of a distinguished family. Beginning in his early teens, he wandered with his family to Fez, Morocco, and the Holy Land, and finally to Cairo, where he settled. Here he became physician and counselor to the Vizier and to the legendary Caliph Saladin. His fame as a physician became so widespread that Richard the Lion-hearted of England invited him to serve as his own court physician—an offer which Maimonides declined. He was soon recognized as the leading Jew of Egypt, and was in active correspondence with Jews through the entire Diaspora, answering questions of law, advising, guiding, and comforting his harassed brethren the world over.

Portrait (1744);
authentic signature

Some searching questions put to him by a former pupil, Joseph ibn Aknin, led to the composition in 1190 of his most famous work, *Moreh Nevuchim* or *Guide to the Perplexed*. In it he deals with problems of theology and the interpretation of Scripture and of Jewish law, which frequently troubled the minds of students of philosophy and religion. His intention again and again was to find a rational explanation for what seemed entirely arbitrary, as, for example, the regulations governing sacrifices and the dietary laws.

Although the "Guide" was written in Arabic, Maimonides used Hebrew characters. Chapter by chapter, he sent it to Joseph ibn Aknin, with the caution not to let any Arab see it for fear of reprisals for what he had to say about Mohammed. Soon, however, it did come to the notice of the Arabs, who were not offended, but on the contrary praised it. Originally published in 1190, it was translated into Hebrew during the author's lifetime by Samuel ibn Tibbon, and later by Jehudah al Harizi. Translations into Latin and European languages followed, and the "Guide" has remained a classic ever since.

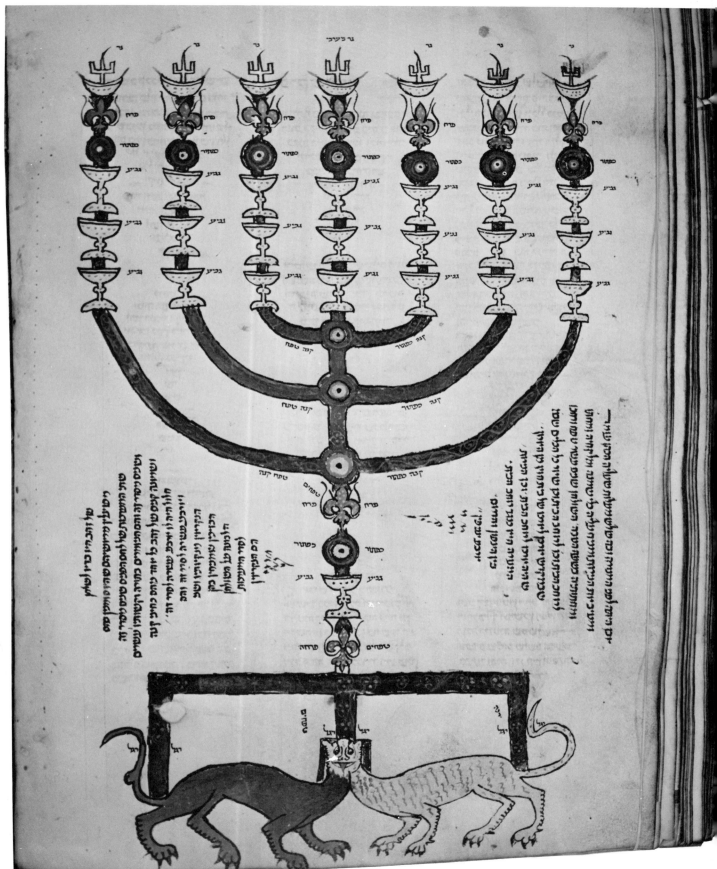

Diagram illustrating Mishneh Torah, Germany 13th centu

Maimonides' handwriting   *Mishneh Torah, Book V*

83

Letter soliciting funds for redemption of captives

Relics of Egyptian Jewry

ELEVENTH-THIRTEENTH CENTURIES

The photograph on the opposite page is a sacred memento of Cairo, Egypt. Once a proud center of Jewish learning and creativity, the Jewish community of Cairo is now almost extinct as a result of Arab hostility and persecutions. The Holy Ark, now in the Jewish Museum of New York, was presented to Dr. Solomon Schechter, scholar, and founder of the Jewish Theological Seminary in New York City. He brought it with him from his "discovery" of the Genizah in the legendary Ezra Synagogue of Fostat, a suburb of Cairo. The synagogue was founded in 616 in a building that had been converted from a church. (It was named Ezra because of a legend that it contained a scroll written by Ezra the Scribe.) The synagogue is reported in the travels of Benjamin Tudela as long ago as the 12th century, and it has been visited by famous travelers through the centuries.

It became especially famous because of its Genizah, the hideaway of discarded sacred Jewish writings to be stored until they could be buried. These worn books, pages, manuscripts, and documents are known as *shemot* which means *names*—in other words, the various mentions of the Divine Name, written or printed on parchment or paper, which may not be profaned by destroying or burning. Dr. Schechter's finds made history—so much so that when we say Genizah today we usually mean the Cairo Genizah. Schechter's collection of some 100,000 items and those of other travelers have kept scholars busy over sixty years studying the literature, history, and life of the Jewish people in the Middle Ages. It is estimated that the hoard of manuscripts will keep students of the Genizah at research, study, and work for another sixty years.

The Prague Altneuschul

TWELFTH CENTURY

Prague, capital of Czechoslovakia, formerly Bohemia, is one of the oldest and most historic of all Jewish communities in Europe. In the sixteenth century it was a spiritual center of world Jewry, distinguished by such figures as *Maharal,* Rabbi Judah Loew (legendary creator of the Golem) and the sainted *Sheloh,* Rabbi Isaiah Horowitz. The Altneuschul is still Prague's oldest synagogue, and thus one of the chief historic monuments of European Jewry. Situated near the old Jewish cemetery, it was probably erected in the eleventh century and renovated about the middle of the twelfth. It is said that the rabbis prohibited its reconstruction and expansion because of the hallowed blood of Jewish martyrs that had been shed on its walls in the pogrom of 1389; nevertheless, it has more than once been rebuilt after being partly burned and demolished by rioting mobs. The building and its interior are gloomy and forbidding.

There are two theories concerning the name of the synagogue. According to one, it originally had the name *Al-t'nai.* There is a legend that it was first built by Jews exiled from the Holy Land after destruction of the Temple in the year 70, on a foundation of stones borne from the Temple. They vowed that when the Messiah came and brought them back to Jerusalem, they would demolish it and once again return the stones to Zion, whence the name *Al-t'nai,* for the Hebrew "on condition." A more matter-of-fact theory is that the name means simply the *Alt-neu* "Old-New" *Schul* or synagogue.

Its simiplicity and proportion render the synagogue one of the gems of early European Gothic architecture. The unknown architect undoubtedly had in mind the synagogue of Worms as a model.

In accordance with the accepted tradition, originally no houses nearby might overshadow it in height. In time, however, it became difficult to maintain this proscription. In the eighteenth century the ancient law was finally set aside after a tower had been added to the nearby town hall of the "Jewish Town."

Rabbinic Responsa

Halakhah, or Jewish legal literature, was until recent times the chief preoccupation of Jewish creative genius. Professor Louis Ginsberg, outstanding Talmud scholar of the recent past, estimated that from the beginning of the Common Era to the eighteenth century fully 78 percent of the literary output of the Jews was *halakhic* in content.

Halakhic literature consists of the Talmud and its commentaries, and the various compilations of codes (outstanding among which are the Mishneh Torah by Maimonides and the Shulhan Arukh by Joseph Karo).

Of significant importance in halakhic literature is also the literature of the She'elot U'tshuvot (questions and answers, most often concerning legal decisions) or responsa. These are written decisions and rulings by leading rabbis and heads of talmudic academies to questions concerning day-to-day matters on various phases of life not covered by the Talmud. The rabbis based their answers on interpretations of biblical and talmudic laws so as to fit the new circumstances and changing conditions. In ruling on matters for which no earlier provision had been made, they tried to apply the spirit as well as the letter of the Law and to indicate the bases in the Talmud from which they developed their reasoning and application.

Responsa are being written to this very day. Over a thousand collections are known to be in existence. They cover nearly eighteen centuries of Jewish life, and are not only a rich reservoir of Jewish law but also an invaluable source of historical information. They contain data on the way the Jews lived in different places at different times, on their relations with the non-Jewish world, their occupations and pastimes, as well as their institutional life.

The responsum reproduced here is from Rabbi Solomon ben Adret, or Rashba, as he is popularly known (1235-1310), a Spanish rabbi who lived in Barcelona and was considered the leader of Spanish Jewry in his time. The halakhic responsa, numbering over three thousand, were not only accepted but highly regarded by later codifiers. They also constitute a valuable record of Jewish life in various Jewish communities in Europe, Africa, and Asia.

כל הפקר ולנוקפ

ני חלי דרך נתן יכן לרד רדין השד

פר הוה הרשעה יהן אוצר ה יוכא לוראה ה והחבי בורר וא אלוי כח עד ולוצר וצא לצר וצמירין אעור

תשובות   שאלות

בשבר וון חוות עכונ לרולקבא
זל כעש כה חה ענולים חוה
עז לחטרר שע עוב חלבו ע
ועי לפחר יחך חוף פך פבר
קוה על עוסן לקני עב (וגוטוע)

The Great Synagogue of Toledo (Santa Maria de la Blanca)

TWELFTH CENTURY

The oldest Jewish monument in the Spanish city of Toledo is the former Great Synagogue, built in the last years of the twelfth century, under the reign of Alfonso VIII of Castile, when the Jews of Spain still lived in freedom. In 1405 there was a massacre of the Jews led by a monk, Vincent Ferrer, and afterward the synagogue was converted into a Catholic church called Santa Maria de la Blanca—the name it bears today.

The outer wall of the building has a modest appearance, in keeping with those around it. The gate opens into a pleasant garden, scented by roses and acacias, with a spring in one corner and a path lined with cypresses leading to the doorway of the building itself.

Inside the edifice one enjoys seeing the lightness and grace of Moorish architecture at its best. Thirty-two octagonal columns, surmounted by elaborately carved capitals in stucco, divide the rectangular space into a series of five arcades. Supported by the columns are horseshoe arches, typical of the Arabic style, decorated with rosettes and medallions. Above the arcades runs a frieze in which geometrical patterns, *fleurs-de-lys,* the Shield of David, and other stylized motifs are charmingly combined. Overhead is a paneled ceiling. Unlike El Transito, another former synagogue turned church, the building contains no Hebrew inscriptions—apparently because the custom of including such inscriptions did not begin in Spain until about 1300, some years after the Great Synagogue was built.

Jews' Court in Lincoln, The Oldest Dwelling House in England

THIRTEENTH CENTURY

The ancient building known as Jews' Court, at the foot of Steep Hill in Lincoln, is one of three buildings that date from medieval times (about the thirteenth century). All three are associated with Jews. One of them, the House of Bellasez the Jewess, is probably the oldest inhabited house in England. Cecil Roth, noted historian, has identified this house as a former synagogue, for a number of reasons. That it was constructed for use as a public building is evident from the large single room on the first floor above street level, which runs almost the entire length and is large enough to seat nearly a hundred people. The building is a little higher than the neighboring house, in accordance with the tradition that the synagogue should be more prominent than the houses that surround it. Although there is no women's gallery, it is supposed that, as was customary in very old synagogues, the women worshipped behind a screen or in an adjoining room. In the east wall, traditionally facing Jerusalem, is a niche measuring 34 by 36 inches where the Ark of the Torah Scrolls was kept.

According to Dr. Roth, the extremely bare-looking entrance is a later addition. He suggests that the original entrance probably looked like the monumental entrance to the House of Bellasez, next door.

On the ground floor, below the synagogue, are rooms which presumably were used for living quarters by the synagogue functionaries and for religious instruction. According to Dr. Roth, "Jews' Court" is the only medieval synagogue building left in England, and is "one of the oldest constructions of the sort in the whole of Europe."

The town of Lincoln is remembered by students of English history and literature for its association with the tragic blood libel associated with "Little Hugh of Lincoln" (1255).

On the ninth of Av (July 18), 1290, the Jews of England were expelled, and with them the sixty-six householders of Lincoln. The thirty houses they owned, together with an enormous amount of booty, were confiscated by King Edward I, and from that day there has been no Jewish community in the town.

93

Tomb of St. Hugh, Lincoln Cathedral

לַחְמָא עַנְיָא דִּי אֲכָלוּ אַבְהָתָנָא
בְּאַרְעָא דְמִצְרַיִם כָּל דִכְפִין יֵיתֵי
וְיֵכוּל כָּל מָאן דְצָרִיךְ יֵיתֵי וְיִפְסַח
הַשַׁתָּא הָכָא לְשָׁנָה הַבָּאָה

The Sarajevo Haggadah

CA. THIRTEENTH CENTURY

Sarajevo, a byword in European history as the scene of the murder that triggered World War I, is also memorable for its connection with the history of Jewish art. In April 1941, during World War II, the Nazis occupied this city in the province of Bosnia, now Yugoslavia. They had orders to seize the Sarajevo Haggadah; it had been hidden away in a mountain village, from which it was returned after the war. Now it is one of the chief treasures of the Bosnian National Museum.

This rare manuscript, one of the great examples of medieval Jewish art, contains the Haggadah or home service for the eve of Passover, including the prayers, psalms, and hymns concerning the Exodus and deliverance of the Children of Israel from the House of Bondage in Egypt.

What makes this manuscript outstanding is the sixty-nine full-page illuminations depicting in vivid detail episodes from the history of the Children of Israel. The drawings, though lacking in proportion, are realistic, and their representations of dress, furnishings, utensils, etc., throw much light on life of the Middle Ages.

It is believed that the Haggadah was written and illustrated somewhere in northern Spain during the late thirteenth or early fourteenth century. Discovered in Sarajevo—hence its name—at the end of the nineteenth century, it has been reprinted several times.

The Oldest Known Yiddish Manuscript

1382

The oldest Yiddish manuscript, a collection of four poems on biblical themes, together with a fable and a poem about a princess, was discovered in 1953 in the Cairo Genizah collection at Cambridge University, England. It bears the date, November, 1382. Until its discovery, the oldest known Yiddish text had been a translation of the Book of Psalms dated 1490.

After its discovery a facsimile of the manuscript was published in two volumes by Brill in Leiden, Holland, under the title *The Oldest Known Work of Yiddish Literature, 1382.* The edition included a translation into German, and a short introduction by Leo Fuchs, director of the Rosenthal Library at Amsterdam, who first identified the language of the manuscript as Yiddish.

Publication of this work caused a sensation among philologists and literary historians. The first question they asked was how a Yiddish text could have found its way into the Cairo Genizah since Jews in Mediterranean countries did not speak Yiddish. Scholars in Germany and the United States have argued that the text, though written in the Hebrew alphabet, should really be regarded as an early example of German literature. Others maintain that although the manuscript contains only one Hebrew word, the spirit of the poems and the approach of the author or authors is entirely Jewish. Furthermore, the entire text is written in consonants only, without vowels, and from internal evidence it is clear that the author or authors wrote it for a Jewish audience.

The four poems on biblical themes retell some of the stories of the Bible, and include material from the Midrash and the Talmud. They exhort the reader to lead an ethical life. A poem about the Garden of Eden expresses the belief that all Jews who have died a martyr's death for their faith will find peace and rest in Paradise. A poem about Abraham speaks of a landscape covered with snow— a familiar scene in Europe though not in the Middle East.

The fable concerns a lion that terrorizes all animals until it is punished by the Creator. Some scholars interpret it as an allusion to a dynasty, possibly that of the Mamelukes, who persecuted the Jews and were eventually destroyed.

The Synagogue of Samuel Ha-Levi (El Transito) in Toledo

FOURTEENTH CENTURY

One of the most beautiful examples of medieval Jewish architecture is the synagogue built in 1366 by Samuel ha-Levi Abulafia, treasurer to Peter I of Castile. Later, when it came into possession of the Jesuits, it was named El Transito.

In shape the building is rectangular, measuring about thirty by seventy-five feet. Unlike the Great Synagogue (now the Church of Santa Maria de la Blanca), it has no central pillars. Around the four walls are fifty-four arches supported by double columns of alabaster. These also frame the windows, some of which are blind and others which admit light through delicate lattices of stone, carved with geometric designs; no two are exactly alike. The decoration shows the influence of Islam (whose artists are forbidden to use animal or human forms) in its strictly stylized clusters of flowers, vines, pine cones, *fleurs-de-lys,* and geometrical patterns.

Under the windows, alternating with a frieze of these designs, are poignantly appropriate verses from the Psalms, including the Eighty-Fourth and the One Hundredth. The Hebrew lettering is among the most perfect of its kind.

In the Abulafia Synagogue the women's gallery is screened off by an open-work lattice of carved alabaster and is reached through a handsomely decorated door. Its walls are ornamented with verses from the Song of Miriam (Exodus XV). The east wall contains the niche where the Holy Ark once stood and carries the date of the building and the names of its donors.

The forty-foot ceiling is of wood from the famous cedars of Lebanon, inlaid with mother-of-pearl, which is now chipping away. This and the Great Synagogue of Toledo are two of the many synagogues that once existed on the Iberian peninsula; they have been preserved because they were converted to be used as churches. Despite the addition of Christian altars, statues, and crucifixes, something of their original Hebraic atmosphere remains even today.

99

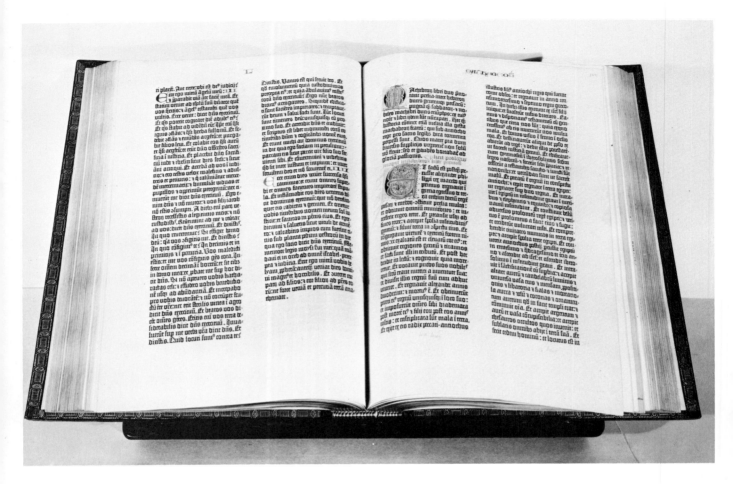

First Page of Psalter, 1457

The Gutenberg Bible

1455

The first book printed from movable type was a Latin Vulgate edition of the Bible, printed by the inventor of printing, Johannes Gutenberg, for whom it was named. The Gutenberg Bible was published (1455) in two volumes of 317 and 324 pages, each page in a double column consisting of forty-two lines each. It was printed in block letters modeled on the cursive script, twice the size of ordinary book type, and had no capital letters. These were added later in the hand of an experienced scribe. The ink used for printing was colored and had an oily base, since inks containing water would not adhere to the metal type.

We are not certain how many copies of Gutenberg's masterpiece were printed. Only forty-six, some on paper and some on parchment, have survived destruction. But there is no question of its beauty, and today it is valued as one of the most precious books in the world.

Earliest portrait of Gutenberg, 1584

Woodcuts: casting type, printing book

The First Printed Hebrew Book

1474

According to the best available knowledge, the earliest printed Jewish book dates February 19, 1474, and appeared in Regiio di Calabria, a little Italian town on the Mediterranean. The first of four volumes, it was a commentary by the beloved medieval scholar and teacher, Rabbi Solomon Itzhaki—or Rashi, as he is popularly known. It was printed by Abraham ben Garton. The second printed Hebrew volume was a book of laws, *The Four Pillars,* by Rabbi Jacob ben Asher; it was produced near Padua, in Northern Italy, by the physician Meshullam Cuzi.

The early printers regarded themselves as teachers rather than businessmen. They were idealists, men fired with a zeal to spread the Word of God. In Amsterdam, for example, one printing firm adopted as its seal or trademark a picture of a priest (the priests, as will be recalled, were the first teachers in Israel) with hands outstretched in the traditional gesture of blessing. Another printer used as his trademark an angel pouring water, symbolic of the tribe of Levi, one of whose duties was to wash the hands of the priests before they blessed the people.

Between 1475 and 1500, at least 150 Hebrew books were printed, each containing a few hundred pages in editions of from 250 to 300 copies. These books are known as incunabula, from the Latin word *cunae,* meaning "cradle," since they were produced while the printer's craft was in its infancy. Such books are very rare and precious. Of the total number of Hebrew incunabula, about two-thirds were printed in Italy and the rest in Spain. Most of them were burned by the Church in its zeal to wipe out the Jewish faith. Only single copies, leaves, or fragments have survived. Such of the incunabula as were salvaged have been preserved mainly in the large libraries of Europe, where they are kept under lock and key.

Rothschild Manuscript

1485

One of the world's masterpieces of calligraphy and painting in miniature is this manuscript, commissioned by a wealthy man whose name is believed to have been Moshe ben Yekutiel Hacohen. It was executed around 1485, probably in the Italian city of Ferrara, by a team of craftsmen who appear to have set up a special workshop for the project. Evidently the contents were specially designated by the commissioning patron; they include the Psalms, the Book of Job, the Ethics of the Fathers, and the Passover Haggadah, as well as a variety of secular books by such authors as Josephus and Aristotle; they add up to a total of forty-seven distinct works. The finished manuscript consisted of nearly five hundred separate leaves, or nearly a thousand pages, of soft vellum, measuring a little over 6 by 8 inches, and all exquisitely lettered, gilded, and illuminated by hand. That the patron came from an Ashkenazic background is evident from the spirit, the work of two or more scribes. The lavish decorations, which include many graceful marginal figures of animals, as well as many useful clues to the daily life of northern Italy in the late fifteenth century, make it one of the most precious of illuminated Hebrew manuscripts.

Now known as the Rothschild Manuscript, it is in the Bezalel National Museum at Jerusalem. The illustration in this book comes from manuscript No. 24.

Abrabanel's Commentary to the Bible

A towering Jeremiah-like figure, Rabbi Isaac Abrabanel belonged to a distinguished family of Spanish Jews who claimed descent from King David. His grandfather and father, who served at the royal court of Seville, later suffered persecution, forced conversion, impoverishment, and exile. From Spain they fled to Portugal, where they once again rose to important positions at the royal court. Don Isaac was born at Lisbon in 1437. He was given a thorough education in Hebrew and the entire range of general studies, including languages, physics, astronomy, and mathematics.

His knowledge of Greek and Latin classics and of the works of Christian and Moslem scholars, as well as of Jewish Bible commentators, led Abrabanel to undertake a new commentary to the Bible. He was not satisfied with those available in his own time. The one by Rashi he thought too brief; others he criticized as too cryptic, too pedantic, or too mystical. He wished to throw light on the unique beauty of the Bible, its spiritual and ethical grandeur. In his work he drew upon his own experiences as statesman, financier, and exile. To each of the books he wrote a long preface concerning the problems of history, philosophy and theology posed by the Scripture. A major move was to defend the Bible against the zeal of certain monks, including apostate Jews, who had tried to twist the words of the Holy Scriptures into an instrument of propaganda aimed at destroying Judaism and gaining converts for Catholicism. He strove also to give comfort to his exiled brethren by strengthening their belief in the ultimate coming of the Messiah.

As a favorite of the Portuguese king, Don Isaac at first had little time for scholarly work. He began to devote himself to his commentary only when, like his forebears, he too was obliged to flee from place to place. In 1483 he moved from Portugal to Spain, where he was soon summoned by Ferdinand and Isabella for financial advice. But nine years later, after failing in his strenuous efforts to thwart the cruel designs of Torquemada, the fanatical Grand Inquisitor, to destroy the Jews root and branch, Abrabanel was among the three hundred thousand Jews who left Spain deprived of all their possessions. At the age of fifty-five he arrived in Naples, where he once again served as financial adviser to the king. When the French conquered that city, he fled to Corfu. Finally he settled in Venice, where he died in 1508 or 1509 at the age of about seventy-two years. Despite all his misfortunes, he was blessed with sons and descendants who carried on the noble name of Abrabanel.

ב

ספר בראשית

הקדמה

פרשת בראשית

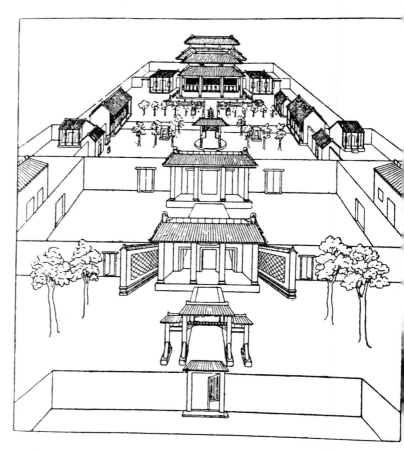

Exterior view of the synagogue

古代開封之

清眞敎史略

Reading the Torah from the Chair of Moses

Kai Feng-Fu—Extinct Chinese Jewish Community

FIFTEENTH CENTURY

Before its extinction, the ancient Jewish community of Kai Feng-Fu, in the Honan province of central China, dated back nearly a thousand years. The community had been unknown until it was discovered by Catholic missionaries in the seventeenth century. A synagogue built there about 1163 had been rebuilt about 1279, again in 1461, and a third time—following destruction by flood—in 1652. Inscriptions found in the synagogue were dated 1489. The synagogue, looking somewhat like a Buddhist temple, had a Chair of Moses where the Torah was read. It also contained incense burners and a special hall for the worship of dead ancestors.

Some two hunded fifty years ago, the Jewish religion of the Kai Feng-Fu community had become a mixture of Confucianism, Judaism, Buddhism and Islam. When the existence of Chinese Jews became known to Western Jewry, efforts were made to communicate with them, but without success. Christian missionaries endeavored to convert them. Rebellions and unrest thwarted contacts with the Jewish world. The last remnants of the Jewish community lived in abject poverty and ignorance. In religious matters they were illiterate. They dressed like the Chinese and wore queues. Originally few in number, they eventually scattered to Shanghai and Hong-Kong. In 1900 the estimated number of Chinese Jews was 140; a few years later they had disappeared altogether.

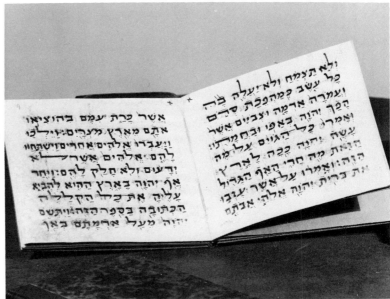

Bible written in Kai Feng-Fu in 17th century.

109

שיר

הַשִּׁירִים אֲשֶׁר לִשְׁלֹמֹה ׃ יִשָּׁקֵנִי מִנְּשִׁיקוֹת פִּיהוּ כִּי טוֹבִים דֹּדֶיךָ מִיָּיִן ׃ **שִׁירִין** וְתוּשְׁבְּחָן דִּי אֲמַר שְׁלֹמֹה נְבִיָּא
מַלְכָּא דְיִשְׂרָאֵל בְּרוּחַ נְבוּאָה

קָרָם רִבּוֹנָא עַלְמָא ײַ עֶשְׂרָם **שִׁירָתָא אִתְאַמְרָא** בְּעַלְמָא הָדֵין שִׁירָתָא דֵין מְשַׁבַּח מִן כֻּלְּהוֹן שִׁירָתָא קַמְיְתָא כְּזִמָּן דְּאַשְׁכְּחִין לֵיהּ חוֹבְתֵיהּ וְאָתָא וְיִכָּא
דְּשַׁבְתָא וְאָגֵין עֲלוֹהִי פָּתַח פּוּמֵהּ וְאָמַר מִזְמוֹר שִׁיר לְיוֹם הַשַּׁבָּת **שִׁירָתָא תִּנְיִיתָא** אֲמַר מֹשֶׁה עִם בְּנֵי דְיִשְׂרָאֵל בְּזִמַּן דִּי בְּזַע לְהוֹן מָרֵי עַלְמָא
יַת יַמָּא וְסוֹף פָּתַח פּוּמְהוֹן כֻּלְּהוֹן וַאֲמָרוּ שִׁירָתָא **שִׁירָתָא תְּלִיתָאָה** אֲמַרוּ מֹשֶׁה וּבְנֵי יִשְׂרָאֵל בְּזִמַּן דְּאִתְיְהֵיבַת לְהוֹן אֵרָא
רָבָא וְדַרְדְּרִין כְּתִיב בְּגִין שַׁבָּחוּ יִשְׂרָאֵל **שִׁירָתָא רְבִיעָאָה** אֲמַר מֹשֶׁה נְבִיָּא אֲנָן קְרָבָא בְּגִבְעוֹן וְקָם לֵיהּ שִׁמְשָׁא וְשֵׁית שַׁעֲתִין וּפָסַק מִלְמֵימַר שִׁירָתָא פָּתַח פּוּמֵהּ
אִיהוּ וַאֲמַר שִׁירָתָא וְרַבְּרְבִין פָּתַח בַּר נֶצַח **שִׁירָתָא שְׁתִיתָאָה** אֲמָרָה חַנָּה בְּזִמַּן דְּאִתְיְהֵיב לַהּ בַּר מִן קֳדָם ײַ קַנְטוֹרֵי כְּתִיב וְצַלִּיאַת חַנָּה בִּנְבוּאָה וַאֲמַרַת
וּמְדִין כְּתִיב וְשַׁבַּח וְדִבְחָה וְקַבַּר נֶצַח צַבְאוֹ **שִׁירָתָא שְׁבִיעָאָה** אֲמַר דָּוִד מַלְכָּא דְיִשְׂרָאֵל עַל כָּל נִסַּיָּא דַּעֲבַד לֵיהּ ײַ פָּתַח פּוּמֵהּ וַאֲמַר שִׁירָתָא וְשַׁבַּח דָּוִד בִּנְבוּאָה קָרַם ײַ **שִׁירָתָא**
מְצַעֲתָא אֲמַר שְׁלֹמֹה מַלְכָּא דְיִשְׂרָאֵל בְּרוּחַ קֻדְשָׁא קֳדָם שַׁלִּיט רִבּוֹן כָּל עַלְמָא ײַ **וְשִׁירָתָא שְׁמִינִיתָא** אֲחִידוֹן לַעֲתִיד בְּנֵי גָּלוּתָא בְּעִדָּן דְּיִפְקוּן מִנֵּי גָלוּתָא וְהַדְבְרוֹן כְּתִיב
וּמְפָרַשׁ עַל יְדוֹי דִי יְשַׁעְיָה נְבִיָּא כְּתִיב שִׁירָא הָדֵין יְהֵא לְכוֹן אַתְקַדָּשׁוֹת חַגָּא וַחֲדוַת לִבָּא כְּעַמָּא דְּאָזְלִין לְאִתְחֲזָאָה קֳדָם ײַ תְּלָת
זִמְנֵי בְּשַׁתָּא בְּמַנֵּי זְמָרֵי וְקֹל טַבָּלָא לְמֵעַל לְטוּרָא דַײַ וּלְמִצְלַי קֳדָם ײַ תַּקִּיפָא דְיִשְׂרָאֵל ׃ יִשָּׁקֵנִי ׃ אֲמַר שְׁלֹמֹה נְבִיָּא בְּרִיךְ שְׁמֵהּ דַײַ דְּיָהַב הַכֹּל אוֹרַיְתָא עַל
יְדוֹי דְּמֹשֶׁה סָפְרָא רַבָּא כְּתִיבָא עַל תְּרֵין לוּחֵי אַבְנַיָּא וְשִׁיתָא סִדְרֵי מִשְׁנָה וְתַלְמוּדָא בִּגְירָסָא וַהֲוָה מִתְמַלֵּיל עִמָּנָא אַפִּין בְּאַפִּין כִּגְבַר דְּנָשֵׁיק לְחַבְרֵיהּ מִן סַגִּיאוּת
חִיבְּתָא דְּחָבֵיב לָנָא יַתִּיר מֹשֶׁבְעִין עַמְמַיָּא ׃ לְרֵיחַ

אַחַת דְּבַר אֱלֹהִים סָתִים זוּ סֵמַעֲנוּ ׃ מִקְרָא אֶחָד יוֹצֵא לְכַמָּה טְעָמִים ׃ וְסוֹף דָּבָר אֵין לְךָ מִקְרָא יוֹצֵא מִידֵי פְשׁוּטוֹ וְחִסַּמְעוּ ׃ וְאַכַּפִּי סַרְבְּרוּ
הַנְּבִיאִים דִּבְרֵיהֶם בְּרוֹמְחָא כָּרִיךְ לְיַשֵּׁב הָרוֹמְחָא עַל אוֹפַנְיָה וְעַל סִדְרָהּ ׃ כֵּמוֹ שֶׁהַתִּיכְרְאוּת סְדוּרִים זֶה אַחַר זֶה ׃ רָאִיתִי לַסֵּפֶר הַזֶּה
כַּמָּה מִדְרָשִׁים חֲבֵרָה יֵשׁ סְדָרִים שֶׁל כָּל הַסֵּפֶר הַזֶּה בְּמִדְרָשׁ אֶחָד ׃ וְיֵשׁ מְפוּזָרִים בְּכַמָּה מִדְרְשֵׁי אֲגָדָה מִקְרָאוֹת לְבָדָם וְאֵינָם מְיֻשָּׁבִים
עַל לְשׁוֹן הַמִּקְרָא וְסֵדֶר הַמִּקְרָאוֹת ׃ וְאָמַרְתִּי בְּלִבִּי לַתְפּוֹס מַשְׁמָע הַמִּקְרָא לְיַשֵּׁב בִּיאוּרֵיהֶם עַל סְדָרָם וְהַמִּדְרָשׁוֹת רַבּוֹתֵינוּ קְבָעְתִּים מִדְרָשׁ וּמִדְרָשׁ אִישׁ אִישׁ בִּמְקוֹמוֹ ׃
וְאוֹמֵר אֲנִי שֶׁרָאָה שְׁלֹמֹה בְּרוּחַ הַקֹּדֶשׁ שֶׁעֲתִידִין יִשְׂרָאֵל לִגְלוֹת גָּלוּת אַחַר גָּלוּת חֻרְבָּן אַחַר חֻרְבָּן וְלְהִתְאוֹנֵן בְּגָלוּת זֶה עַל כְּבוֹדָם הָרִאשׁוֹן וְלִזְכֹּר חִבָּה
רִאשׁוֹנָה אֲשֶׁר הָיוּ סְגֻלָּה לוֹ מִכָּל הָעַמִּים לֵאמֹר אֵלְכָה וְאָשׁוּבָה אֶל אִישִׁי הָרִאשׁוֹן כִּי טוֹב לִי אָז מֵעַתָּה וְיִזְכְּרוּ אֶת חֲסָדָיו וְאֶת מַעֲלָם אֲשֶׁר מָעֲלוּ וְאֶת טוֹבוֹת אֲשֶׁר אָמַר
לָתֵת לָהֶם בְּאַחֲרִית הַיָּמִים ׃ וְיִסֵד סֵפֶר הַזֶּה בְּלָשׁוֹן אִשָּׁה צְרוּרָה אַלְמְנוּת חַיּוּת מִשְׁתּוֹקֶקֶת עַל בַּעֲלָהּ מִתְרַפֶּקֶת עַל דּוֹדָהּ מַזְכֶּרֶת
אַהֲבַת נְעוּרֶיהָ אֵלָיו וּמוֹדָה עַל פִּשְׁעֶיהָ אַף דּוֹדָהּ צַר לוֹ בְּצָרָתָהּ וּמַזְכִּיר חַסְדֵי נְעוּרֶיהָ ׃ וְנוֹי יָפְיָהּ וְכַשְׁרוֹן פְּעָלֶיהָ אֲשֶׁר בָּהֶם נִקְשַׁר עִמָּהּ בְּאַהֲבָה עַזָּה לְהוֹדִיעָהּ כִּי
לֹא מִלִּבּוֹ עִנָּהּ ׃ וְלֹא שִׁלּוּחֶיהָ שִׁלּוּחִין ׃ כִּי עוֹד הִיא אִשְׁתּוֹ וְהוּא אִישָׁהּ ׃

שִׁיר הַשִּׁירִים אֲשֶׁר לִשְׁלֹמֹה ׃ סָם רַבּוֹתֵינוּ כָּל שְׁלֹמֹה הָאֲמוּרִים בְּשִׁיר הַשִּׁירִים קֹדֶשׁ מֶלֶךְ שֶׁהַשָּׁלוֹם שֶׁלּוֹ ׃ שִׁיר מַהוּ עַל כָּל הַשִּׁירִים אֲשֶׁר נֶאֱמַר
לְהַקָּבָּ"ה אֲמָרָם עַמּוֹ וּכְנֶסֶת יִשְׂרָאֵל ׃ אָמַר רַבִּי עֲקִיבָא לֹא הָיָה הָעוֹלָם כְּדַי כַּיּוֹם שֶׁנִּתַּן בּוֹ שִׁיר הַשִּׁירִים לְיִשְׂרָאֵל שֶׁכָּל הַכְּתוּבִים קֹדֶשׁ
וְסֵדֶר הַמִּדְרָשׁ קֹדֶשׁ הַקָּדָשִׁים ׃ אָמַר רַבִּי אֶלְעָזָר בֶּן עֲזַרְיָה לְמָה הַדָּבָר דּוֹמֶה לְמֶלֶךְ שֶׁנָּטַל סְאָה חִטִּין וּנְתָנָהּ לְנַחְתּוֹם אָמַר לוֹ הוֹצֵא לִי כָּךְ
וְכָךְ סֹלֶת כָּךְ וְכָךְ אַבְנִין כָּךְ וְכָךְ מוּרְסָן וּסֹלֵק לִי מִתּוֹכָהּ גְּלוּסְקָיָה אַחַת מְנֻפָּה וּמְתוּלָה ׃ כָּךְ כָּל הַכְּתוּבִים קֹדֶשׁ וְשִׁיר הַשִּׁירִים קֹדֶשׁ קָדָשִׁים שֶׁכֻּלּוֹ יִרְאַת שָׁמַיִם
וְקַבָּל עֹל מַלְכוּתוֹ וְאַהֲבָתוֹ ׃   יִשָּׁקֵנִי מִנְּשִׁיקוֹת עַל"א

The First Rabbinic Bible

1517

Mikraot Gedolot, or rabbinic Bibles, were first printed in the sixteenth century. They were so called because the Hebrew text of certain books was accompanied by the Targums or translations into Aramaic; the rabbinic commentaries such as those of Rashi, Levi ben Gerson, Rabbi David Kimchi, and Nachmanides, among others; and the Masorah. The first such Bible (without the Masorah) was the work of Felix Pratensis of the Augustinian Hermits, a Christian religious order; it was published by Daniel Bomberg at Venice in 1517. Bomberg, a non-Jew and native of Antwerp, was the first printer to bring out the entire Talmud, as well as the first publisher of a rabbinic Bible. After he established his press at Venice in 1516, he had the distinction of doing more to spread Jewish learning than any other printer of his time. Felix Pratensis was the son of a rabbi, a student of classical philosophy as well as of Hebrew. He taught Daniel Bomberg Hebrew, and it was his influence that led Bomberg to set up a Hebrew press.

Pratensis began his work on the biblical text by comparing and collating many manuscripts. He wrote that he was restoring the Hebrew to its "true and original splendor." His critical edition, with its notes and comments, served as a basis for the second *Mikraot Gedolot,* and had a far-reaching influence on later printings of the Bible, both in Hebrew and in translation. His edition is the first in which the books of Samuel, Kings and Chronicles are each divided into two parts, and in which Nehemiah is separated from Ezra. It is also the first to indicate the numbers of the chapters in Hebrew characters.

שער יהוה החדש

ארך ימים בימינה בשמאלה

עשר וכבוד · דרכיה דרכי נעם וכל

זהו מישר מה שהדפסנו בזיבור זה · ראשונה החומש
עם תרגום ופי׳ רש״י ן׳ עזרא : והנביאים ראשונים
עם פי׳ רש״י וקמחי ור״לבג : והנביאים האחרונים
ישעיה עם פי׳ רש״י ואבן עזרא · ירמיה ויחזקאל עם
פי׳ רש״י וקמחי · תרי עשר עם פי׳ רש״י ואבן עזרא :
והכתובים תלים עם פי׳ רש״י ואבן עזרא · משלי עם
פי׳ אבן עזרא ור״לבג · איוב עם פי׳ אבן עזרא ור״לבג ·
דניאל עם פירוש אבן עזרא ורבינו סעדיה גאון ·
עזרא עם פי׳ אבן עזרא ורש״י · דברי הימים עם פי׳
מיוחס לרש״י · חמש מגלות עם פירוש רש״י ואבן
עזרא · והמקראות מתורגמים מנוקדים ומוטעמים
ומסרים על פי דרכי הסופרים קדמונינו אנשי כנסת
הגדולה והסופרי׳ הבאים אחריהם אשר על מסלולם
ומסלולם דרכנו בבנין אותיות תלויות וקטנות וגדולות
ועקומות וניקוד פרבה על הכתב וכתב פרבה
על הניקוד וסתומו׳ ופתוחות וכתוב ולא
נקרא ונקרא ולא נכתב ואותיו׳
מנוזרו׳ כל אלו מוגים
עם רב העיון
כפי כח
המפסר והדפסי
במצות
דניאל יצ״ו בן קרניאל בומבירגי
ז״ל פה ויניציאה הבירה בסייעתה דשמיא :

נתיבותיה שלום · עץ

חיים היא למחזיקים בה ותומכיה מאשר

(U2347)

Mikraot Gedolot

SECOND RABBINIC BIBLE
1516-17

Until the twentieth century the so-called second rabbinic Bible was the standard printed edition of the *Tanach* or Holy Scriptures. It is called in Hebrew *Mikraot Gedolot,* or Great Scriptures, and in English the rabbinic Bible, because in addition to the Hebrew text it includes the Targum (Aramaic translation of the Bible) and such leading rabbinic commentaries as those of Rashi (Rabbi Shlomo Itzhaki), Rabbi Abraham Ibn Ezra, and Radak (David Kimchi). It was printed in 1524-25 by the Venetian, Daniel Bomberg, a Christian, who engaged a Tunisian Jewish scholar, Rabbi Jacob ben Hayyim, to make a comparative study of the existing manuscripts on which the latter based his text. A special feature of the Bible is the inclusion of the Masoretic notes and variant readings in the manuscripts studied by Rabbi Jacob.

As stated on p. 111, the first rabbinic Bible was produced by Felix Pratensis, and was also printed by Daniel Bomberg in 1516-17. Because the editor was a Jew who had converted and became a Christian monk, his work was proscribed in Jewish homes and schools. Bomberg was persuaded by Rabbi Jacob ben Hayyim to do a second edition, which benefited from the work of his predecessor. The second rabbinic Bible had far-reaching effect on Bible translations in the western world. It became the standard Hebrew text and served among others as the basis for Luther's translations and the King James version.

אלו

דברים שאין להם שיעור הפאה והבכורים
והראיון וגמילות חסדים ותלמוד תורה אילו
דברים שאדם אוכל פירותיהן בעולם הזה

Bomberg type face

ורבי יהודה מכשיר בגמרא מפרש טעמייהו כלבנדרייהו במתחי
וסוכה גבוהה מסרה בגמרא מפרש טעמייהו סלם
רפסתא כמי בגמרא וליף להו׃ וסוכה שאינה מרובה

מאי

שהיו שבח מרובה פסולה

שהיא גבוהה למעלה מעשרים אמה פסולה
ורבי יהודה מכשיר ושאינה גבוהה עשרה
טפחים ושאין לה שלשה דפנות ושחמתה
מרובה מצילתה פסולה׃ גמ׳ תנן
התם מכני שהוא נבוה מעשרים אמה ימעט
רבי יהודה אומ׳ אינו צריך מאי שנא גבי סוכה
דתני פסולה ומאי שנ׳ גבי דתני תקנתא
סוכה דאוריתא תני פסולה מבוי דרבנן תני
תקנתא ואיבעית אימא בדאוריתא נמי תני
תקנתא מיהו סוכה דנפישי מילה פסיק ותני
פסולה מבוי דלא נפישי מילה תני תקנתא
מנא הני מילי אמר רבה דאמ׳ קרא למען ידעו
דורותיכם כי בסוכות הושבתי את בני ישראל
עד עשרים אמה אדם יודע שהוא דר בסוכה
למעלה מכ׳ אמה אין אדם יודע שדר בסוכה
משום דלא שלטא בה עינא רבי זירא אמ׳ מהכא
וסוכה תהיה לצל יומם מחורב עד עשרים אמה
אדם יושב בצל סוכה למעלה מעשרים אמה
אין אדם יושב בצל סוכה אלא בצל דפנות
אמר ליה אביי אלא מעתה העושה סוכתו
בעשתרות קרנים הכי נמי דלא הוי סוכה אמר
ליה התם דל עשתרות קרנים איכא צל סוכה
הכא דל דפנות ליכא צל סוכה ורבא אמר
מהכא בסוכות תשבו שבעת ימים אמר׳ תורה
כל שבעת הימים צא מדירת קבע ושב בדירת
עראי עד עשרים אמה אדם עושה דירתו דירת
עראי למעלה מעשרים אמה אין אדם עושה
דירתו דירת עראי אלא דירת קבע אמר ליה
אביי אלא מעתה עשה מחיצות של ברזל וסיכך
על גבן הכי נמי דלא הוי סוכה אמר ליה הכי
קאמינ׳ לך עד עשרים אמה דאד׳ עושה דירתו
דירת עראי כי עביד ליה דירת קבע נמי נפיק
למעלה מעשרי׳ אמה דאדם עושה דירתו דירת
קבע כי עביד ליה דירת עראי נמי לא נפיק
כולהו

The First Printed Talmud

1519

The first complete edition of the Talmud was published in Venice by the Christian printer, Daniel Bomberg. He began work on it in 1519, starting with the tractate *Pesahim* (Passover), and pursuing the task vigorously and without interruption until the spring of 1523, when he completed the last tractate, *Taharot* (Purification). The printing of books in those days required special permission from the government and church authorities. The few who were granted the privilege were closely supervised to make sure that there was no derogation of God, Jesus, King, or Church.

The printing of the Talmud occurred during the turbulent days of Protestant Reformation led by Martin Luther, a revolt which the Dominican Order was especially active in attempting to suppress. For years they had shown their fear of the Talmud by burning precious manuscripts which had been confiscated from the Jews and carted to the pyres in wagon loads. For centuries the Church had opposed talmudic and rabbinic literature, lest it encourage criticism of Jesus and Christian doctrine. Against this background, the permission given by Pope Leo X to print the Talmud, was a victory for humanism and enlightenment and a historic step in the march toward religious freedom.

Orach Chayim, last page, printed by Abraham Conat, 1476

בראשית

בראשית ברא : ברא אלהים את השמים ואת הארץ

אמ' ר' יצחק לא היה צריך להתחיל
את התורה אלא מהחדש הזה לכם שהיא מצוה ראשונ' שנצטוו ישראל ומ"ט פתח בבראשית
משום כח מעשיו הגיד לעמו לתת להם כח אם יאמרו האומות לישראל לסטים אתם
שכבשתם שבע' ר'בנות ורצונך יהם אומרים להם של כל הארץ של הקב"ה היא ברא' ונתנה לאשר ישר'ב
בעיניו כרצונו נתנה ל'הם וברצונו נטלה מיה' ונתנה לנו ' בראשית ברא ' אין המקרא הזה א
אומר אלא דורשני כמו שדרשו רבותינו בשביל התורה שנקראת ראשית דרכו ובשביל ישראל
שנקראו ראשית תבואתו ' ואם באת לדרשו כפשוטו כך פרשהו ' בראשית ברייַת שמים וא
רץ ' והארץ היתה תהו ובהו וחשך ' ויאמר אלהים יהי אור ' ולא בא המקרא להורות סדר ה
בריאה לומר שאלו קדמו שאם בא להורות כך היה לג לכתוב בראשונה ברא את השמים וגו'
שאין לך ראשית במקרא שאינו דבוק לתיבה של אחריו ' כמו בראשית ממלכת יהויקים '
ראשית ממלכתו ' ראשית דגנך ' אף כאן אתה אומר בראשית ברא אלהים את השמים ' כ
כמו בראשית ברא כלומר בברא וד'ומה לו תחלת דבר ה' בהושע ' כלומר תחלת דבורו של
הקבה'כהושע ויאמר ה' אל הושע וגו' ' ואם תאמר להורות בא שאלו תחלה נבראו כברא'שי
כל ברא את אלו ' יש לך מקראות שמקצרים לשונם וממעטי ' תיבה אחת כמו כי לא סגר דלתי
בטני' ולא פירש מי הסוגר ' וכמו ישא את חיל דמשק ולא פירש מי ישאנו ' וכמו יעבד ראשי'ת
אחרית דבר ' אם כן תמה על עצמך שהרי המים קדמו ' שהרי כתיב ורוח אלהים מרחפת מ
על פני המים ' ועדיין לא גלה המקרא ברייַת המים מתי ' מכאן למדת שקדמו ברייַת המים
לארץ ' ועוד שהשמים מאש וממים נבראו ' על כרחך לא למד המקרא בסדר המוקדמי ' ו
והמאוחרים כלום ' ברא אלהים ' ולא אמ'ד

Soncino Books

The Bible, Talmud, and prayerbook printed by the Soncino family, most eminent Jewish printers of the fifteenth century, bear the name of a town near Milan, in northern Italy. Here the family established their first press in 1483. As typical of medieval times, three generations of the family worked at the establishment, under supervision of the founding grandfather. Originally the family had come from Germany, the country of Gutenberg. With the rise of the Soncino Press, four generations of the family wandered with their printing equipment to places as distant as Venice, Italy; Salonika, Greece; and Constantinople, Turkey. Although they printed non-Jewish works in Latin, Greek, Italian, and other languages, their greatest fame rests on their printings of the Bible and the Talmud. In the first edition of the Soncino Bible the ineffable four-letter name of God, Y'H'W'H, was printed "Y H W D," and *Elohim* (God) as *Elodim,* so as not to take the Holy Name in vain (Exodus XX:7). Such was the painstaking pride in their work, that they took as their slogan a paraphrase of Isaiah II:3: "For out of Zion shall come forth the Law and the word of God from Soncino."

Being a printer in the early days required not only expert technical knowledge but extensive learning and high integrity. Gershom Soncino, most famous of his family, traveled the world over in search of accurately worded manuscripts for setting into type and printing.

The Soncino trademark achieved the highest reputation for accuracy, beauty, and high quality. A generation ago an organization was founded in Germany to revive interest in Hebrew printing and to produce beautiful Jewish books; it called itself the Soncino Society. Unfortunately it was destroyed by the Nazis along with most of Europe's Jewry and Jewish cultural treasures.

Soncino seal

Soncino type face

וְכַפְתֹּר תַּחַת שְׁנֵי הַקָּנִים מִמֶּנָּה וְכַפְתֹּר
תַּחַת שְׁנֵי הַקָּנִים מִמֶּנָּה וְכַפְתֹּר תַּחַת
שְׁנֵי הַקָּנִים מִמֶּנָּה לְשֵׁשֶׁת הַקָּנִים הַ יֹ
הַיֹּצְאִים מִן הַמְּנֹרָה: כַּפְתֹּרֵיהֶם וּקְנֹתָם
מִמֶּנָּה יִהְיוּ כֻּלָּהּ מִקְשָׁה אַחַת זָהָב
טָהוֹר: וְעָשִׂיתָ אֶת נֵרֹתֶיהָ שִׁבְעָה וְהֶעֱלָה
אֶת נֵרֹתֶיהָ וְהֵאִיר עַל עֵבֶר פָּנֶיהָ:

Tab eclipsis luminariuz et primo de sole

numer⁹ annoruz	nomina mensiuz	dies	digiti	feria	bore	minut	finis eclipsis hore	minu
1493	octob	10	9	5	0	0	1	20
1502	septēb	30	8	6	17	28	19	12
1506	Julii	20	3	2	1	49	3	3
1513	martii	7	4	1	23	49	1	9
1518	Junii	7	10	2	18	22	19	17
1524	sanuar	23	9	2	3	12	4	6

Tabla de eclipsib⁹ lune

numer⁹ annoruz	nomina mensiuz	dies	digiti	feria	bore	minut	finis eclipsis hore	minu
1494	septēb	14	17	1	17	5	2	33
1497	ianuar	18	17	4	3	50	7	18
1500	nouēb	5	13	5	10	17	13	30
1501	maii	2	19	1	15	33	19	6
1502	octob	15	14	7	10	15	12	9
1504	februã	29	16	5	10	47	14	13
1505	aug⁹	14	15	5	5	42	9	6
1508	Junii	12	23	2	15	21	19	0
1509	Junii	2	7	7	9	29	2	3
1511	octob	6	13	2	9	11	2	25
1514	ianuar	29	15	2	14	20	16	3
1515	ianuar	19	15	7	5	0	6	42
1516	Julii	13	14	1	10	0	12	30
1519	nouēb	6	20	1	5	50	6	48
1522	septēb	5	15	6	11	22	12	4
1523	martii	1	17	1	7	30	9	14

Zacuto's Astronomical Tables

Abraham ben Samuel Zacuto (also known as Diego Rodrigo), astronomer and rabbinical scholar, was born in Salamanca, Spain, about 1450, and died in Damascus about 1525. He served as professor of astronomy at the universities of Salamanca and Saragossa. Zacuto was author of an important work on astronomy, which was translated into Spanish and Latin and which played a part in the discovery of the New World and the opening of new sea routes. Zacuto also drew up improved astronomical tables which were used by Columbus; a copy with annotations by the discoverer is preserved in Seville. Indeed, Columbus' writings mention how he saved himself and his crew from trouble with the Indians by predicting an eclipse with the aid of Zacuto's tables.

Zacuto shared the fate of his brethren when given the choice of converting to Catholicism or expulsion from Spain. He chose the latter. Like the family of Abrabanel, he emigrated to Lisbon, Portugal, where he was appointed royal astronomer to King João I. Vasco da Gama, Alfonso de Albuquerque, and other Portuguese explorers used his astronomical tables. In Lisbon Zacuto's activity was at a peak. Here he worked out a new astrolabe in iron instead of wood. The invention was of great value to the Portuguese maritime explorers and navigators, especially da Gama, who used it in exploring the sea route to India.

But Zacuto, along with his fellow Jews, did not long find peace in Portugal. He settled in Tunis, where he wrote his well-known *Sefer Yuhasin,* printed posthumously in Constantinople, 1566.

In this, the work that brought him immortality in Jewish literature, he gives an account of the transmission of the Oral Law. He records the history of the kings of Israel and Judah, as well as of neighboring nations and of the Jews up to his own period.

Little is known of Zacuto's later life, or when and where he died. But like his contemporaries he wandered through many cities; we know that in 1513 he was in Jerusalem and in 1515 in Damascus.

Zacuto's signature

Tráſ.Gre.lxx.cũ interp.latina.　Tráſla.B.Dic.　Tex.heb.Joſue.ca.j.Pꝛitiua.he.

9

IOSVE.
ΙΗΣΟΥΕ.

Incipit liber ioſue.
Cap.j.

A

Et factũ eſt poſt　mortē moy
Αἰ ἐγένετο μετὰ τὴν τελευτὴν μωυ
ſi ſerui dñi:　τ locut eſt dñs
ſῆ δ᾽ ούλου κυρίου, κὴ εἶπε κύριος τῶ
ioſue filiũ nũ	miniſtro moyſi
Ἰησοῦ υἱῷ ναυὴ τῷ ὑπουργῷ μωυσῆ

dices:moyſes	ſeruus meus moꝛtuus eſt:nunc igſ ſur
λέγων, μωυσῆς ὁ θεράπων μου τετελεύτηκε, νῦν οὖν ἀνα
gẽs tranſi iordanẽ tu τ ois pplis hic in
ſὰς διάβηθι τὸν ἰορδάνην σὺ κὴ πᾶς ὁ λαὸς οὗτος εἰς

Deut. .11. c.

terrã:ꝗ ego do eis. ois locus ad quẽ ãbulauerit
γῆν, ἣν ἐγὼ δίδωμιαὐτοῖς. πᾶς ὁ τόπος ἐφ᾽ ὃν ἐὰν ἐπιβῆ τὰ
veſtigia pedũ vſoꝛ:vobis dabo eũ:	ſicut τ
ἴχνη τῶν ποδῶν ὑμῶν, ὑμῖν δώσω αὐτόν, ὃν τρόπον εἴ
cut ſum moyſi.	deſerta τ	antilibanũ vſqʒ ad
κεν σῶ μωυσῆ. τὴν ἔρημον κὴ τὸν ἀντιλίβανον ἕως τοῦ
fluuiũ	magnũ fluuiũ euphrate: oẽ trã
ποταμῶ τῶ μεγάλω ποταμοῦ εὐφράτου, πᾶσαν τὴν
etheoꝛ	vſqʒ ad mare	a ſolis oc
ἑταίων κὴ ἕως τῆς θαλάσσης τῆς μεγάλης, ἀφ᾽ ἡλίου δυ
caſu erũt termini vſi.	nõ reſiſtet	hõ co
κασμῶ ἔςαι τὰ ὅριαὑμῶν. οὐκ ἀντιςήσεται ἄνθρωπος κα
ram	vobis cũctis	diebus vite tue. τ
ραμ ὑμῶν πάσας τὰς ἡμέρας τῆς ζωῆς σου. κὴ
ſicut fui cum moyſe: ita ero τ tecum
ρ τρόπον ἤμην μετὰ μωυσῆ, οὕτως ἔσομαι κὴ μετὰ σοῦ,

Infra. 5.b.
Heb.13 a.

τ nõ derelinquã te: neqʒ deſpiciam te:cõortaſ τ
κὴ οὐκ ἐγκαταλείψω σε, οὐδ᾽ ὑπερόψομαί σε, ἴσχυε κὴ
eſto robuſtus.tu ẽ diuides	ppſo huic terrã:
ἀνδρίζου, σὺ γὰρ διελεῖς τῷ λαῷ τούτω τὴν

B

quã iuraui	pſibus coꝛ vt tradere eis.ꝯſortare
ἣν ὤμοσα τοῖς πατράσιν αὐτῶν δοῦναι αὐτοῖς. ἴσχυε

Infra co.
Deut. 31.b.
5.Re.2 a.

igſ τ eſto robuſtus:vt cuſtodias τ	facias ſicut pre
οὖν κὴ ἀνδρίζου, φυλάσσεσθαι κὴ ποιεῖν καθότι ἐνε
cepit tibi moyſes ſeruus meus. τ nõ declinabis
τείλατό σοι μωυσῆς ὁ παῖς μου. κὴ οὐκ ἐκκλινεῖς
ab eis	ad dextrã vel ad ſiniſtrã:	vt intelligas in cũctis
ἀπ᾽ αὐτῶν εἰς δεξιὰ κὴ εἰς ἀριστερά, ἵνα συνῆς ἐν πᾶσι
que feceris. τ	nõ recedet	liber
οἷς ἐὰν πράξῃς. κὴ οὐκ ἀποστήσεται ἡ βίβλος τοῦ
legis huius de	oꝛe tuo:	τ medita
νόμου τούτου ἐκ τοῦ στόματός σου, κὴ μελετή
beris in eo	die ac nocte:	vt intelligas facere
σεις ἐν αὐτῷ ἡμέρας κὴ νυκτός, ἵνα συνῆς ποιεῖν
oia	ꝗ ſcripta ſunt in eo.	tũc proſperabis
πάντα τὰ γεγραμμένα ἐν αὐτῷ. τότε εὐοδωθήσεις
vias tuas:	τ tũc intelliges. ecce pꝛecis
τὰς ὁδούς σου, κὴ τότε συνήσεις. ἰδοὺ ἐντέλλο

ĩeo.

pio tibi:cõfortare τ eſto robuſtus: nõ timeas ne
μαί σοι, ἴσχυε κὴ ἀνδρίζου, μὴ δειλιάσῃς

C

oʒ terrearis: qꝛi tecum dñs	deus tuus in
μηδὲ φοβηθῇς, ὅτι μετὰ σοῦ κύριος ὁ θεός σου εἰς
oẽ locuꝗuo preteris. τ	precepit io
πάντα τόπον οὗ ἐὰν πορεύῃ. κὴ ἐνετείλατο ἰη
ſue	ſcribis pplo dices: tran
σοῦς τοῖς γραμματεῦσι τοῦ λαοῦ λέγων, εἰσελ
ſite per mediũ	caſtroꝛ pplo:	τ
θετε κατὰ μέσον τῆς παρεμβολῆς τοῦ λαοῦ, κὴ
imperate	pplo dicẽs:	eſtote parati in ci
ἐντείλασθε τῷ λαῷ λέγοντες, ἑτοιμάζεσθε ἐπὶ ci
barijs: qꝛi adhuc tres dies	τ vos tran
βαρίοις, ὅτι ἔτι τρεῖς ἡμέρας, κὴ ὑμεῖς διαβαί
ſitis iordanẽ hunc:	intrantes τ poſſideba
σετε τὸν ἰορδάνην τοῦτον, εἰσελθόντες κατασχεῖν
terrã:quã dñs	deus	patrũ vſoꝛ
τὴν γῆν, ἣν κύριος ὁ θεὸς τῶν πατέρων ὑμῶν
bat vobis τ.	ruben τ	gad τ dimidie
δώσω ὑμῖν. κὴ τῷ ρουβὴν κὴ τῷ γὰδ κὴ τῷ ἡμίσει

Nu.32.
b. τ infra 4.c.

tribui manaſſe ait ioſue: mementote ſemonis dñi:quẽ
φυλῆς μαναςσῆ εἶπεν ἰησοῦς, μνήσθητε τὸ ῥῆμα κυρίου, ὃ

IStactũ ē poſt moꝛ
tẽ moyſi ſerui dñi
vt loqueretur dñs
ad ioſue filium nun
miniſtrum moyſi:& di
ceret ei. Moyſes ſeruus
meus mortuus ē. Surge
& trãſi iordanem iſtum
tu & ois pplis tecũ: Ter
ram quam
ego dabo filiis iſrael.
Omnem
locũ ꝗuẽ calcauerit veſti
giũ pedis veſtri:
vobis tradã:ſicut locu
tus ſum
moyſi. A deſerto & liba
no vſqʒ ad
fluuiũ magnũ euphratẽ
omnis terra
etheorũ vſqʒ ad mare
magnũ cõtra ſolis occa
ſum erit terminus veſter.
Nullus poterit vobis re
ſiſtere cunctis diebus vi
te tue. Sicut fui
cum moyſe:ita ero tecũ
non dimittam
nec derelinquã te. Con
fortare & eſto robuſtus.
Tu enim ſorte diuides
populo huic terrã. pro
qua iuraui patribus ſuis
vt traderem eam illis.
Cõfortare igitur & eſto
robuſtus valde:vt cuſto
dias & facias oẽ lege
quã pcepit tibi moyſes
ſeruus meus. Ne declies
ab ea ad dexterã vel ad ſi
niſtrã:vt intelligas cun
cta ꝗ agis. Non recedat
volumẽ legis huius abo
re tuo:ſed meditaberis i
eo diebus ac noctibʒ:vt
cuſtodias & facias
oia ꝗue ſcripta ſunt ĩ eo.
Tunc diriges
viã tuã:& intelliges eã
Ecce pcipio tibi:cõfor
tare & eſto robuſtus. No
li metuere & noli tiere:
qꝗtecũ & dñs deus tuus
in oibus ad ꝗcũꝗ prexe
ris. Precepit ioſue pri
cipibus pplis dices: Tran
ſite p mediũ caſtrorũ:&
impate pplo ac dicite.
Preparate vobis ciba
ria:qꝗpoſt diem tertiũ
tranſibitis iordanem:&
intrabitis
ad poſſidendã terrã quã
dñs deus veſter
daturus eſt vobis. Rube
nitis quoqʒ & gadditis
& dimidie tribui manaſ
ſe ait.
Mementote ſermonis
quem

וַיְהִי אַחֲרֵי מוֹת מֹשֶׁה עֶבֶד יְהוָה　הָיָה

וַיֹּאמֶר יְהוָה אֶל יְהוֹשֻׁעַ בִּן נוּן　שָׁרַת

מְשָׁרֵת מֹשֶׁה לֵאמֹר מֹשֶׁה עַבְדִּי　מוֹת

מֵת וְעַתָּה קוּם עֲבֹר אֶת הַיַּרְדֵּן הַזֶּה

אַתָּה וְכָל הָעָם הַזֶּה אֶל הָאָרֶץ אֲשֶׁר

אָנֹכִי נֹתֵן לָהֶם לִבְנֵי יִשְׂרָאֵל כָּל　קוּם

מָקוֹם אֲשֶׁר תִּדְרֹךְ כַּף רַגְלְכֶם בּוֹ　גֵּעַ

לָכֶם נְתַתִּיו כַּאֲשֶׁר דִּבַּרְתִּי אֶל　דָּבַר

מֹשֶׁה מֵהַמִּדְבָּר וְהַלְּבָנוֹן הַזֶּה וְעַד　גָּבַל

הַנָּהָר הַגָּדוֹל נְהַר פְּרָת כֹּל אֶרֶץ　בּוֹא

הַחִתִּים וְעַד הַיָּם הַגָּדוֹל מְבוֹא הַשָּׁמֶשׁ

יִהְיֶה גְּבוּלְכֶם לֹא יִתְיַצֵּב אִישׁ　הָיָה גְּבַל

לְפָנֶיךָ כֹּל יְמֵי חַיֶּיךָ כַּאֲשֶׁר הָיִיתִי　יָצַב פָּנָה

עִם מֹשֶׁה אֶהְיֶה עִמָּךְ לֹא אַרְפְּךָ　יוֹם חָיָה

וְלֹא אֶעֶזְבֶךָּ חֲזַק וֶאֱמָץ כִּי אַתָּה　רָפָה

תַּנְחִיל אֶת הָעָם הַזֶּה אֶת הָאָרֶץ　עָזַב

אֲשֶׁר נִשְׁבַּעְתִּי לַאֲבוֹתָם לָתֵת לָהֶם　נָחַל

רַק חֲזַק וֶאֱמַץ מְאֹד לִשְׁמֹר לַעֲשׂוֹת　שָׁבַע נָתַן

כְּכָל הַתּוֹרָה אֲשֶׁר צִוְּךָ מֹשֶׁה עַבְדִּי　עָשָׂה

אַל תָּסוּר מִמֶּנּוּ יָמִין וּשְׂמֹאול לְמַעַן　צָוָה

תַּשְׂכִּיל בְּכֹל אֲשֶׁר תֵּלֵךְ לֹא יָמוּשׁ　סוּר יָמַן

סֵפֶר הַתּוֹרָה הַזֶּה מִפִּיךָ וְהָגִיתָ בּוֹ　שְׂמֹאל סוּם

יוֹמָם וָלַיְלָה לְמַעַן תִּשְׁמֹר לַעֲשׂוֹת　הָגָה

כְּכֹל הַכָּתוּב בּוֹ כִּי אָז תַּצְלִיחַ אֶת　שָׂמַר מָתַר

דְּרָכֶךָ וְאָז תַּשְׂכִּיל הֲלֹא צִוִּיתִיךָ חֲזַק　צָלַח

וֶאֱמָץ אַל תַּעֲרֹץ וְאַל תֵּחָת כִּי עִמְּךָ　שָׂכַל חָתַת

יְהוָה אֱלֹהֶיךָ בְּכֹל אֲשֶׁר תֵּלֵךְ וַיְצַו　צָוָה

יְהוֹשֻׁעַ אֶת שֹׁטְרֵי הָעָם לֵאמֹר עִבְרוּ

בְּקֶרֶב הַמַּחֲנֶה וְצַוּוּ אֶת הָעָם לֵאמֹר　מָתַת

הָכִינוּ לָכֶם צֵדָה כִּי בְּעוֹד שְׁלֹשֶׁת　מִן צוּד

יָמִים אַתֶּם עֹבְרִים אֶת הַיַּרְדֵּן הַזֶּה לָבוֹא　יוֹם בּוֹא

לָרֶשֶׁת אֶת הָאָרֶץ אֲשֶׁר יְהוָה אֱלֹהֵיכֶם　יָרַשׁ

נֹתֵן לָכֶם לְרִשְׁתָּהּ וְלָראוּבֵנִי וְלַגָּדִי

וְלַחֲצִי שֵׁבֶט הַמְנַשֶּׁה אָמַר יְהוֹשֻׁעַ　חָצָה

לֵאמֹר זָכוֹר אֶת הַדָּבָר אֲשֶׁר　זָכַר

a

The Complutesian Polyglot Bible

1514-17

Polyglot Bibles are a distinct category in which parallel columns of translations are printed alongside the original Hebrew text, as an aid to critical study of the texts, by comparing the translations with each other and with the original. None is the work of a Jewish printer or editor. The oldest is the so-called Complutesian Polyglot, named after the place where it appeared, edited in six volumes by Francisco Ximenez, Archbishop of Toledo and founder of the trilingual University of Alcala in Spain. (The Latin name for Alcala was Complutum—hence the title.) It was completed in 1517, but was not published until 1522, because the papal authorization for its publication had been delayed. It represents the greatest technical achievement, equipment, and skill used on any Bible up to its time.

The three columns on each page consist of the Hebrew, the Septuagint (Greek) and the Vulgate (Latin). The Targum of Onkelos (Aramaic) is added on the bottom with a Latin translation. (The interest in the language of the Targum was due to the fact that it was the vernacular spoken in the days of Jesus.)

Almost simultaneously (1516) appeared the Genoa polyglot Psalter consisting of Hebrew, Greek, Arabic, Targum Onkelos, and a gloss or commentary in Latin. The commentary on Psalms XIX:7 made this polyglot historic, since it was the first to mention the startling discoveries of Christopher Columbus (see 11th and 12th line from the bottom). The translation reads:

Therefore, Christopher, surnamed Columbus, by nationality from Genoa, was one who in our time by his efforts in a few months explored more of land and sea than (scarcely) all the rest of mankind in all past centuries.

121

Shlomo Molcho: Pseudo Messiah

CA. 1525-1530

Shlomo Molcho (1500-1532) was born in Portugal and named Diogo Pires; he was a Marrano or New Christian. As a young man he enjoyed high distinction as royal secretary at the high court of justice. In 1525, when David Reubeni, a self-proclaimed Messiah, arrived in Portugal as ambassador of the Jewish ruler of Khaibar, Arabia, Molcho fell under his influence. His imagination was fired by the romantic tales of the Ten Lost Tribes, the fanciful stories of the travelers Eldad Hadani and Benjamin of Tudela. He was stirred by the mysticism of the time and by the messianic dreams. (These were the agonizing years after the Spanish expulsion.) Returning openly to Judaism, he circumcized himself with his own hands and fled Portugal to avoid persecution. He settled in Salonika, Greece, where he joined a kabbalistic study group. For a time Molcho also lived in Safed, in the Holy Land, which was the center of Kabbalah. In 1529 he published a book announcing the arrival of the Messiah in 1540.

When Molcho learned about the occupation of Rome by troops of the Holy Roman Emperor Charles I, he left for that city; he was convinced that the fall of Rome foreshadowed the arrival of the Messiah. By this time (1529) he had come to regard himself as the Messiah. He lingered for thirty days at the bridge of the Tiber, dressed in rags and living among beggars to exemplify the messianic legend. He later proclaimed the imminent appearance of the Messiah in the synagogue at Rome. His proclamation and behavior made him suspect by the all-powerful Inquisition. Molcho fled to Venice in 1530, where he again met Reubeni. Aroused by Molcho's visionary utterances the Inquisition arrested him (Molcho) and condemned him to be burned at the stake. He was rescued by Pope Clement VII, who allowed him to flee to Germany. There Molcho and Reubeni were received by Emperor Charles I, whom they tried to persuade to organize an army of Marranos to wrest the Holy Land from the Turks. By order of the emperor, however, they were arrested and sent to Mantua, Italy, where they were handed over to the Inquisition. Molcho, condemned to be burned at the stake, was promised a pardon if he would return to Christianity. He spurned the offer and in his thirty-second year died a martyr.

Molcho's signature

Shown here is Molcho's mantle, on display at the Prague Museum. Apparently Prague Jews of an earlier era had rescued it from oblivion. The mantle is woven of brocade and embroidered with gold and silver. It is draped on a large sized mannequin. His banner carried the words in Hebrew, *Mi Kamocha b'Elim Adonay?* ("Who is like unto Thee among the mighty, O Lord"—the initials and slogan of the Maccabees). Molcho carried this banner when he visited the temporal and spiritual leaders of Europe with his messianic message.

שֶׁבֶת

הַמּוֹרֶדֶת עַל הַגּוֹיִם ׃
אֲשֶׁר לֹא יָדְעוּ וְעַל
הַמַּמְלָכוֹת אֲשֶׁר
בְּשִׁמְךָ לֹא
קָרָאוּ ׃

שְׁפֹךְ עֲלֵיהֶם זַעְמֶךָ וַחֲרוֹן
אַפְּךָ יַשִּׂיגֵם ׃ תִּרְדּוֹף בְּאַף
וְתַשְׁמִידֵם מִתַּחַת שְׁמֵי יְיָ ׃

Prague Haggadah

1527

The most complete as well as the oldest of illustrated Passover Haggadahs was printed at Prague by Gershon ben-Solomon Ha-Kohen and his brother Gronem in 1527. The first known book of its kind, it consists of 85 pages, three enclosed in decorative borders, illustrated with 60 quaint woodcuts which reflect the spirit of the late Middle Ages. The Prague Haggadah served as prototype for others that followed, notably the Mantua edition of 1560.

The illustrations and ornamentations reflect the artistic climate of the communities in which Haggadahs were printed. And the craftsmen who illustrated these Haggadahs may be considered the first Jewish artists of modern times.

The Haggadah was reproduced in a facsimile edition by B. Katz and H. Loewe at Berlin in 1926.

בָּבָא דְאַנְטוֹנָא

הייסט דש בוך אין הושש נֵי
טרעבֿט · מן קעבט וואו
אוֹיה בחורש נֵי
מעבֿט :
אין ווארדן
נֵידרוקט
בו
אייזנה אין דער שטאט · אוב
אֵלִיָה הַמְחַבֵּר אִיז נֵויך
דש פרט :

The Bovo Buch

1545

The *Bovo Buch* is the name of a classic of early Yiddish literature, written in Padua in the year 1507 by the Hebrew grammarian, lexicographer, and scholar Elijah (Bahur) Levita (1468-1549). Levita was born and educated in Germany, but in 1496 he left for Italy, where he worked as a proofreader and taught Hebrew to Christian scholars. Among the latter was Cardinal Egidio of Viterbo, in whose house he lived from 1514 to 1517.

Levita wrote poetry in Yiddish, and his translation of the Book of Psalms into Yiddish in 1545 is an important work in the early literature of that language. But he is best known for his novel, the *Bovo Buch,* which became one of the most popular of Yiddish books and was reprinted many times. Its popularity was such that the title became a byword; any fantastic story was called a "Bobe Maaseh"—an erroneous construction meaning literally a tale told by a grandmother, a "bobe."

The Bovo Buch was an adaptation from a popular Italian tale, *Buovo D'Antona,* which in turn had been adapted from a twelfth century tale originating in France. It tells the story of a queen married to an elderly king, to whom a son, Bovo, is born. Later the queen and her lover kill the aged king, and plan to poison Prince Bovo. Upon discovering the plot Bovo escapes disguised as a servant. He meets a princess who falls in love with him even though she supposes him to be a servant. After many hair-raising adventures Bovo finally marries her, returns home, avenges the death of his father, and is crowned king.

The kingdom of the Bovo Buch is a pagan one, some of whose people are Jews. Although the rulers are pagans, many times the author appears to forget this, and has them act and talk like Jews. The novel is full of Jewish expressions and Hebrew words, and the holiday celebrations by the pagans are Jewish in content and spirit. The whole work is still a pleasure to read.

Maharal Tombstone in the Prague Cemetery

SIXTEENTH CENTURY

The Jewish cemetery at Prague is in the center of the Old Town, and lies on the boundary of the ancient ghetto. It is packed with ancient, weathered tombstones of various shapes and sizes. The ground of the cemetery is uneven. Since the space was small and since it is forbidden to exhume old graves in order to use the space, earth was brought in whenever necessary to provide a new layer for additional graves. Thus in some spots there are as many as twelve layers, one above the other. Indeed, this historic graveyard is a "chronicle in stone."

One of the most celebrated memorials in it is the tombstone of *Maharal,* the famous Rabbi Judah ben Bezalel Loew (abbreviated in Hebrew as Ma-Ha-Ra-L). Also known as Der Hohe (chief) Rabbi, Judah Loew was born in Posen about 1513, and died in Prague in 1609. Before coming to Prague he had been Chief Rabbi of Poland. A teacher of famous rabbis and the writer of many commentaries on rabbinic literature and on the Talmud, he was held in the highest regard as the "Glory of the Exile" and the "Light of Israel." But his fame with the masses rests on the legend that he made the Golem out of clay from the river Moldau, and gave it life by use of a charm that bore the ineffable four-letter Name of God.

At Rabbi Loew's behest the Golem protected the Jews against the enemies who accused them of using Christian blood for Passover and who made other malicious and fantastic accusations. When the Golem became uncontrollable and a possible menace to the community, Rabbi Loew took away the amulet and left it forever after a heap of clay.

The theme of the Golem has been treated by many famous writers in Hebrew, German, Yiddish, and other languages. The story has been dramatized on the stage in many parts of the world and has also been filmed.

On top of the Maharal's tombstone lies a heap of pebbles, evidence that even to this day Jews, both humble and well-to-do, visit the grave to pay homage, to pray, and to offer petitions.

A majestic statue of Maharal stands before Prague's city hall. During the Nazi regime it was hidden away and then restored.

Statue of Rabbi Loew

Pinkas of the Council of Four Lands

CA. 1550

The Council of Four Lands (*Va'ad Arba Aratzoth*) was the central body of Polish Jewry from the last quarter of the sixteenth century to the middle of the eighteenth. The Four Lands were Central Poland, Little Poland, Ruthenia (Podolia and Galicia), and Volhynia. Lithuania, too, was included for a time. The *Va'ad* (council) consisted of representatives of the *kahal(s)* (local organized communities), which were autonomous.

In 1549 the King of Poland introduced a poll tax on all the Jews of the realm. In order to collect the tax the Polish government authorized creation of this central body. In time the organization took on other duties, serving as an organ for dealing with mutual problems as a court of appeals, for coordinating relations with the government of Poland, and for regulating the internal affairs of Polish Jews.

The members of the council met twice a year, in the summer in Lublin, Poland, and during the winter at Jaroslaw in the province of Galicia.

The Chmielnicki massacres in 1680 and the general turmoil and unrest that followed in Poland weakened the Council. It was finally abolished by the government in 1764. However, the local communal organizations remained, and they took over the tasks of the central body.

The Council kept a record book (*pinkas*) in which all activities, resolutions, and orders were written down. Although this record was lost, many of the resolutions and decrees and proclamations were either copied down in local record books or quoted in various publications. These materials were collected by Israel Heilpern and published by the Bialik Institute at Jerusalem in 1945.

The first published edition of the pinkas or record book of the Lithuanian Council by Professor Simon Dubnow, distinguished historian, appeared at Berlin in 1924.

Dona Gracia Nasi

1556

This bronze medal, according to Cecil Roth, in the book *Great Jewish Portraits in Metal* (published by Schocken Books for The Jewish Museum of New York), is the first known and loveliest medal of the Renaissance period. On it is the name of Gracia Nasi in Hebrew; in Latin is added her age as 18. There are two theories about the subject of the medal. One is that Dona Gracia (Mendes) Nasi (ca. 1510-1569), a noblewoman, scion of a distinguished banking family, was born as a Marrano in Portugal and became one of the leading women of Europe. She mingled with royalty, was an active international business woman and patron of letters. Known as the "Angel of the Marranos," she helped her fellow Marranos to escape from Portugal and resettle in Europe and Turkey.

Arrested in Venice, she was rescued by the Sultan of Turkey, and she then settled in Constantinople, carrying on daily contacts with her brethren throughout the world. She was one of the most noble and self-sacrificing humanitarians, giving of her wealth and of herself to help the persecuted, homeless, Spanish and Portuguese refugees find new homes. For a short time Dona Gracia lived in Ferrara, Italy, where the medal was struck in 1556. If the face is of Dona Gracia then the artist may have used a portrait of her when she was eighteen, for she was some 30 years older at the time it was done. Another theory is that the subject is that of her niece and namesake. If so, the medal may have been struck in commemoration of the niece's open adoption of Judaism. It is also possible that it was struck to celebrate her marriage to Don Samuel Nasi, brother of Don Joseph Nasi, Duke of Naxos.

The Nasi family played a prominent role in the contemporary Jewish world.

2.º Proceso gr.ª

Luis de Carauajal moço soltero reconci=
liado por este S.to officio por judaicante, residente en
Mexico natural dela Villa de Benauente en Castilla
hijo de Fran.co Rodriguez de Matos y de doña Fran.ca de
Carauajal biuda su muger, de generac.on de Christianos
nueuos de judios

     2.º proceso.   Judaicante relapso per=
                        tinaz,

Ynformacion

Mandado prender

Presso   a   a   a   **Abogado**

Moniciones. 1. 2. 3.

Acussacion

Aprueua
con pu.co   &G   Alcan.de D.or Diony.o de R. g.s lores
g. diffam.

                             Votado

Luis De Carvajal, Mexican Jewish Martyr

1596

Reproduced here is the flyleaf of the published proceedings of the second trial of Luis de Caravahal el Mozo (the Younger), who was burned at the stake in Mexico City on December 8, 1596, with his mother and three sisters, by the Office of the Holy Inquisition. The original is in the National Archives of Mexico.

An uncle of Luis was a Spanish naval captain, who had defeated an attempt by the English to invade the Spanish colony of Mexico. In token of his gratitude, the king raised him to the rank of admiral and made him governor of northern Mexico, with the right of naming his successor. Being himself childless, the governor persuaded his sister, with her husband and family, to immigrate to Mexico, with the understanding that Luis el Mozo would succeed him. The family accepted, partly in the hope of escaping the cruelty of the Spanish Inquisition.

Luis the Younger knew of and took part in his parents' secret practice of Judaism, of which the uncle was unaware. He had an unusually good memory, and as a result of his studies of the Bible he became intoxicated with religion. Soon his gifts made him the recognized head of part of the family.

The family's troubles began when Luis's eldest sister, Isabel, began to be courted by a captain whose family had been Jewish. In her own zeal, she tried to bring her suitor back to the faith. This was her own and her family's undoing. She was arrested by the Inquisition. In fear of arrest and torture, the family fled; some returned to the Old World, where one of Luis's brothers gained fame as a doctor, another as a rabbi. Luis, on his return to Mexico, was arrested and put in prison. During his imprisonment he was subject to visions which had a strong influence upon him. After his release he was able to continue secretly as the spiritual leader of his people throughout New Spain and brought many apostates back to Judaism. Once again, however, he was informed upon, and the whole family was arrested. During a two-year imprisonment he wrote a testament of faith, and composed prayers expressing his readiness to undergo *Kiddush Hashem*—martyrdom to sanctify the name of God. He knew that he was doomed to die at the stake for having lapsed into Judaism a second time.

Together with forty-five other Jews, he was burned at the auto-da-fé in Mexico City. For decades after the event, prayers composed by Luis Carvajal were recited by Mexican Jews.

בריאה ארליא זיין דיא ווייבר ווארדן נשטראפט נ"וייט (דם
בידרות אול (דם בתולים) דש איאיר צער' דאש אנדר
דא טראנט דז קינד מיט איאטאן' דז דריטאיז ווען זיא נאיוטב
קינד האט מאכצאבר צער' אול דיא קלה איז ווס דא איז דיא
בריא ווארדן ור צולוכט דאש זעלבין האבין אלי ווייבר אלו
איכש אלך ווי'אבאודר איבן שר ווי'באם ה' האבין די דריא ברורות
מש העולטאיר נישט קין עושר דר וויל די ברוא האט איום
זולין עבירה נעטאן' אבר דיא קלה ווס אדם איז ווארדן ור
צולוכט דז זעלבין האבן נייארט דיא בוארן אול שלעכטי לייט
איאמון מיט שווייס עשין איר ברוט אבר דישראים אול עלים
דיא האבן דיא קלה ניט' אול מיר נעפינדן דאש עט ווייל אום
נ"ווענט דש דיא ווייבר בון דען שרים אול עלים אודר רייכי
לייט דיא נעבן ווילשווערער צוקינד דרום וויל זיא ניט האבן דיא
קלה בון שווייס עשין ברוט דא האבין זיא די קלה בון טרן
אול קינדר נעוונען פיל מער' אברא'ין ברוא דיא דא ארבייט
דיא האט נערינג קינדר דר וויל זיא האט דיא קלה בון שווערי
ארבייט דא טוט איר הקב"ה חסד מיט שוורער קינדר דש זיא
נערינג קינדר האט' (ואל אישך תשוקתך) אול וויא וואל
דאך דז ברוא איז אונטר טאן דעם מאן זיא מוא איהם פאלגן
וואש ער שפט עליך זו איין קנעכט צו דעם הערין דא וואר
מש בילוך דז דיא ברוא זאלט קיין לושט האבן צו דעם מאן נאך
עליך וואל האט דיא הקב"ה נעגעבן דז זיא אום לושט הבין צו אירם מאן
אול בינערט דש דער מאן זאל הערשן איבר איר אונ איהן זער
איבר וויבי קנעכט' (ולזלה אשת עשה השדה) איז וייא דיא
עבירה' האבן נעטאן דא האבן זיאן'עטשן אלי דיא עט קריעטר
אוש דעם נארטן אול בון דער ברוא עבירה אן אול ווייטר דא האט
הקב"ה זר ווערט איז צו עשין אוש דעם נארטן ניבארט וואש
דא וואקשט אויף דעם פעלד' (בזיעת אמיך האכל לחם)
מיט שווייס אול שווערי ארבייט דען זאלט זיא ניט האבין דיא
עבירה נעטאן זיא האבין נעפונטן האבן נעטשן וויין און נעמאכט
מעלט זיא האבין נשטימקט אלש עט ברוט' אול (דער (בזיי)
שרייבט עינד ארליא צער מוא דיא ברוא ליידן (דם נידות)
אול (דם בתולות) אול שוורער טראגן אול שוער נעוויכן אול
דש זיא אוו לושט האבן צואירם מאן דז זיא איך אצטער איז'בון
דש וועגן אול דז עט ער איבר איר שבט דען דער וויל זיא האט
נעבאטן אויך אדם ער זול עשין בון דעם אפיל דרום נעבט דער
מאן איבין איבר אור אול שבט איבר איר ז' (ואל אישך
תשוקתך) אין דער צייט ווען דיא ברוא נול צו קינד נעט דא
אנט זיא אול ווי זאל איך ווידר קומן צו מיינם מאן די צרות הב
איך בון איהם דא זאנט הקב"ה דיא זולשט דיא ווידר הבן נרושן
לושט מער אלש מער' ער זאנט רבי'ברכיה אול רבי סימון בון
וועגן רבי שמעון בן יהואי איטטאיר'נבדר אין אירם העראנצי
ווילניט מער קומן צואירם מאן דר וויל זיא שווער צוקינד נט
דרום אום זיא איין קרבן ברענגן אול זיא'אויך שטט אוי ז' דר
קינדר בעטאיין כתרה אול אירם גבדראושךאי'צבדרדרט ניט דר
מאן אויך צו דר (ספר תורה) ומען נ'איו דעם קינד בעט נט
דש זאל זיין איין כתרה אויך דעם וויל דעם אויך אירק אבדר דש זיא

איום הערבן האט נעבט נ'יוט האט נ'יט הרוים'נערעט דען נ'ברב
(ויקרא שם אשתו חוה) דער וויל חוה איז נ'ווענא דיא אוטר
בון אלי דיא לייט דרום האט זיא'אדם איין נאמין נעבן חוה דאש
איטטייטש דז לעבין בון דער נבי וועלט אול וויא וואל דאך דש
ער הוט פאר איין נאמן נעבן צו חוה זיא האט זיא ג'היישן אשה
ג'יארט אדם דער האט זיך נ'דאכט דער וויל איין וויל זיין האט
עבירה נעטאן אול האט מיך נ'מלכ עבירות טן דא ווי'אלך איך'איז
ביט מיהסה זיין נאך מיר דען פאר האט'זיא'יא ניהיישן אשה דר
וויל זיא פון מיר איז ווארדן נ'מון אבר אי'גבדרט אום איך
איר איין אנדרן נאמין נעבן אול אם זיא היישן חוה דארום
וויל דיא ווייבר פ'יל רידן דען דש ווארט חוה איזט טייטש רידן
אול בון דעם פ'יל רידן ווי'אוורדן דיא'אוטר בן אולטר בון'אל דער
וועלט דען זאלט זיא ניט פיל האבין נ'רעט מיט דער שלנג דא
ווער זיא ביט טוט דיא אוטר נ'וונן בון אל דער וועלט' (ויעש
אלהים לאדם ולאשתו כתנות עור) הקב"ה דר מלב'ט'אעדר
נ'אדם הראשון אול צו זיינם, וויב אול אויך דעם העאר'איזט
וואלט נ'ווען אול דאש אוי'נעבהט אלי דיא חיוה'אל דיא פעגל אין
דעם עולם אול דער האט זיא'וויער נ'נעבן צו'קין (ואל דא קין
איטטוווארדן דער שלאנן דא זיין ניקומאן הבט (נמרוד)
אול דא (עשיו) האט דר שלאנן (נמרוד) דא נאם (עשיו) דיא
וועלבינע קליידר דא (יעקב) האט וועלן נ'ין צו (יצחק) דיא
ברכות בעמין דא האט יעקב אן נ'טאן דיא וועלבינע קליידר
(ולבישם) אול וויא וואל דאך דש זיא האבן עבירות נ'טאן
נאך עליך וואל האט'איטט דיא הקב"ה דר ברית אול זיא'וועלברט אן
ניקליידט דיא'בהעאדרי' (וישלחהו'י אלהים מגן עדן לעבוד
את האדמה אשר לקח משם ויגרש את האדם) הקב"ה דער
האט'אדם איז דעם (עדן) אול נ'ארין אול לאקרין דער'נער
ווער ניט ארויש נ'גבן ויל ווען אין אול אויל עליך הבן דר שלאנן מיט
אלי יאירתא'אול הקב"ה וואלט ניט'אין ער וועלין דר שלאנן דר'אל
דרום הוט הקב"ה ברוך הוא נ'יאנ'אל אדם אוש דו'אושט דר'ערבן
דיא ערד אוש דעם נ'טאן בישט נ'ראן וורדן אול אז דיא ערבטשט אין
דעם עדן דען דיא בישט ג'ווען ואורדןאיור דער'ערד דיא
דא איז'אויר דעם נ'אן עדן כ'ודנ'ינע אדם אוי דעם נן'אדן צו
ארבייטן ער נ'דאכט ער'וויל ווידראריין קומן אבר הקב"ה דר
פאר שלוט דיא'יטיר בון דעם נן עדן דש ער ניט קונט ווידר
הריין קומן' (וישכון מקדם לגן עדן את הכרובים) הקב"ה
דער האט אלין די'א (מלאכי חבלה) רואן אול האבן אין קארי
הענד בלוסי מעסיר אול שוורט דש קין ביש'עפ'אבנש אלט
ניט קומין אין דאש נ'עדן (והאדם ידע את חוה אשתו)
אול אדם דר האט בישלאפנין וויב חוה אול דארום וויל דר
זרע בון דעם מעלבן קואטאיו דעם מנחו'וואו דער שלאל אול
חלמא איז דארום האט דיא תורה אן נ'שריבן דש בייא דעם שלופן
אין (לשון ידע) ווא דער שלאליש אול דארום דא אדם הט
נ'וונהן דש דז נ'שטן אייט'וורדן ור שלאפין דא האט זיא ערי'ניט
נ'וואלט לענ'בייא'איהם וויא'אוז ער אם מיין קינדר ווערדן ניט
קומן אין דאש נ'עדן ניאירטאין דאש נ'יהנם' דאהאטער
נ'עבהן דש זיא נ'הבן אומין דא'אנעט ער דר וויל זש נ'הבן אול'הן
איטט

Tze'enah U're'enah

1600

"Go forth, O ye daughters of Jerusalem . . ." (*Song of Songs III*:11.)

This is the name given to a Yiddish version of the Five Books of the Torah and the Haftarah (the weekly selection from the Prophets that follows the portion of the Torah chanted in the synagogue), specially compiled for women. It includes a paraphrase of the Five Books, interwoven with material taken from the Midrash and post-biblical commentaries. The *Tzenah U're'enah* was also popularly known as the *Taitch* (a corruption of the word Deutsch or German) *Chumash* (the word in Hebrew for Pentateuch). Written in a simple, informal style, but with great piety, it was read on the Sabbath by generations of Jewish women and was often given as a bridal gift. The *Taitch Chumash* went through numerous editions— estimated at 300—and was published in many countries, including the United States.

The originator of the *Tzenah U're'enah,* Rabbi Jacob Ben Isaac Ashkenazi, was born in Janow, Poland in 1550, and died in Prague in 1626. He was a maggid or itinerant preacher, who knew how to move his audience. The first edition was published in 1600. The oldest edition now extant is that of 1622, printed at Basel, Switzerland.

Portion of an early edition of Tze'enah U're'enah with woodcut illustrations.

Ari Synagogue

SIXTEENTH CENTURY

Safed, a town of narrow, crooked, cobbled lanes, rises 2700 feet above sea level in the mountains of Upper Galilee. Not far away, at Meron (see p. 54), is the tomb of Simon Bar Yohai, the reputed author of the *Zohar* or "Book of Splendor," a commentary on the Five Books of Moses. Permeated with mysticism and with expectation of the coming of the Messiah who was to redeem the Jewish people, the *Zohar* became the fountainhead of the Kabbala, a set of occult doctrines that flourished during the Middle Ages. In Palestine, Safed became the center of a small group of Kabbalists founded and led by the Holy Ari, for whom the Ari Sephardic Synagogue is named.

Entrance   *Ark*

Originally constructed around the end of the sixteenth century, the synagogue may be seen today at the upper edge of the town as one goes toward the mountainous region beyond. The location is said to have been chosen because of the Ari's custom of going for walks with his pupils into the mountains. One of the unusual features of the synagogue is a small vaulted cave that opens off the southeast corner of the main building, and to which according to tradition the Ari withdrew for study and contemplation. Another notable feature is a well in the women's section, which is still used.

The Holy Ari was born Isaac Luria Ashkenazi, at Jerusalem in the year 1534. As the surname suggests, his family had migrated there from Germany; the name Ari, which means "lion" in Hebrew, is an acrostic for *Adonenu* (literally, Our Master) Rabbi Isaac.

In 1569 the Ari went to Palestine, where he settled in Safed and was regarded as a saint. The move came during a cataclysmic period in Jewish history, when the Jews had been expelled from Spain and Portugal, and when their sufferings as a result of persecution had become intense. In Safed the Ari's disciples, who included both mystical scholars and men of simple faith, established a penitential community, delving deeply into ethical questions, practicing charity, observing the Sabbath with special devotion, and purifying themselves with the intent of hastening the Messiah's coming and the redemption of Israel.

The teachings of the Kabbala awakened Jewish people everywhere, leading to still other pseudo-Messianic movements. The most noted of the Ari's disciples were Rabbi Hayim Vital, who was responsible for the spread of his teachings, and Rabbi Joseph Caro, author of the *Shulhan Arukh* (literally, "Prepared Table"), the code that governs Jewish religious practice to this very day. The Ari himself became a legendary figure. His vision of welcoming the Sabbath as a bride dressed all in white was commemorated in the *Lekha Dodi,* composed by one of his followers at Safed, and beloved by Jews everywhere as the hymn sung at Friday evening services to welcome in the Sabbath Queen:

"Come, O friend, the bride to meet
Come, O friend, the Sabbath to greet."

מסכת שבת פרק ראשון

א מעשה גשאך מן מײנט תלמיד חכם דער האט מל
זין טאג ניקט מגררטט גטאן נמרט טאג
מול נאלט גילערנט מול ער שטורב מוז גאר זײן יונג פון
ימרן · דם נאמן זײן ווײב זײן טלית מול תפילין מול גינג
מין דם בית המדרש לו דען רבנים · מול זאמן ווידר
דען רבי עט שטיט גשריבן מין דער הײליגי תורה
(כי היא חייך ואורך ימיך) דמט מיז טײטט דיר רײן
טעג · נון אין ואמן דער האט טאג · מול זים דר לענגט דיר דײן
טעג · און אין ואמן דער האט טאג · מול נאלט ניקט
מנדרטט גטאן גילערנט · ווארום מיז ער דען מוז
יונג פון ימרן גשטורבן · דם וואר ניאנט מין בית המדרש
דער מיר דרוין קאנט ענטפרן · זײא וואוסטן מיט מאמת
קײן טעג ניט · וארום ער מוז מוז חדר גשטארבן · ניט
לאנג דר נאך קאם מײן תלמיד חכם דער האט אים גוט
מיבר נעכאלט · דם זאמנט זים מיט מיז דיא שאעה · דם
פרעגט ער דיא פרוים · ליבה פרוים למז מיך דיך
פרעגן ווי זײן דיא אלן בײם דיר גהאלטן ווען דום
ביסט נדה גוועזן · דם זאמנט זים מיט מיר דער חם וטולף
דו ער איך זמולט מן גרירט האבן איט דען קלײנן
פינגר · מײ זא ער טוייגן דט ער זמולט עפיט מגררטט איט
איר גטמן האבן · דם פרעגט ער גאר מין וועלכם דינג
מול דמז פון מײן תלמיד חכם העט · דם פרעגט ער אים ווידר
זאמן איר זים האבן עט זמול מיט מוכנר אם רן גיהערט
אבר זי ווען וויטערט ניקט · דא גינג דער שטן ווידר
פר הקב"ה מול שפרמך הער מל דער וועלט דיא מיך האב
זמולט מוין גאלט ערד אם בן עארם האב זײם גיבן · דם
גינג דר שטן לו מאטה רבינו מול שפרמך מוטה דיא
תורה דיא דיר הקב"ה גגבן האט וואו האטטו זים
הין גטמן · דם שפרמך מוטה רבינו מל אים קואוטטו
לו איר מול פרמגשט נאך דיא תורה מער בין איך
מער וומז בין מיך דט אין מיר תורה האב געלטט דיא
תורה גיבן · ווים נון הט מיר השם יתברך זעלטט דיא
רבינו ניט זמולט גשטין דז ער דיא תורה האט אקבל
גוועגן · שפרמך הקב"ה דוא ביסט מײן לינגר ומרום
לײקנעסט דו מיך דיר דיא תורה גגבן האב · דם זאמנט
מוטה הער מול דער וועלט מין זעלטט גוטטיג כל מול
דיא תורה מיז דיר דם אלט מין אונזטיג לוסטיג וען
ער דם מרום לערנט · מול דם רוא דיך מול טאמן מעלברט
דרין דר אײמטט מול לערנטט מול זעלברט רחיים · מל
מיך זאל איך דר הלבן דרויך בריאן · מול זאל זאמן מיך

א א א ה ב

מסכת שבת פרק רבי עקיבא

ב מעשה גשאך ער זאמנט רבי יהושע בן לוי מין דער
לײט דם הקב"ה האט דים תורה גגבן

Maaseh Book

1602

Maaseh in Hebrew means "deed." Etymologically it has come to mean "story." *Maasebücher* were story books of the Middle Ages, in which tales, legends, and parables concerning the heroes of Jewish life, biblical, talmudic, medieval, were collected. Originally published in Germany, about the beginning of the fifteenth century, in an early form of Yiddish, they were designed to exhort and teach women and young people through entertaining accounts of exemplary heroic personalities. The Judaeo-German in which they were composed was the forebear of modern Yiddish and was printed in Hebrew characters. Although originally intended for women and girls, who were not duty bound to study the Bible and Talmud, they soon became popular among the men folk as well.

The first Maasebücher also dealt with non-Jewish themes such as King Arthur and his knights and the *Nibelungenlied* (see *Bovo-Buch*).

A Maasebuch published in Basel in 1602 contained some three hundred *maasim,* derived and adapted from the Gemara, from the Sefer Hasidim, Sefer Musar (Ethics), and the like. Each story begins "A *maaseh* happened" or "There was a *maaseh* once upon a time." The stories are permeated with noble and lofty ideals; told in a style which is naive but filled with deep religious feeling. They have been translated into English by Moses Gaster, and are available in the Schiff Classics issued by the Jewish Publication Society of America.

Inscriptions of names of concentration and death camps

Pinkas Synagogue (Prague)

1625

At the edge of the ancient Jewish quarter in the city of Prague, scarcely a stone's throw from the Altneu Synagogue and the town-hall, stands the ancient Pinkas Synagogue. Explorations show that it is built upon foundations dating as far back as the ninth to eleventh centuries, and that prior to 1365 a building known as Pinkas stood on the site. The synagogue stone structure dates back to 1625.

The name is most probably derived from a man's name—Pinhas (Phineas); in Czech, Pinkas. Or it may come from the word in Hebrew for a record book for official minutes of important events, contributions and the like.

After World War II the Pinkas Synagogue was converted into a museum by the Czechoslovak Government. It now houses permanent exhibitions of objects and documents describing the Nazi atrocities from the years 1938 to 1945, and the fate of the Jews in Czechoslovakia at the time of the Nazi occupation—their segregation from the rest of the population, their deprivation of civic rights, their degradation and deportation to the death camps. The documents testify to the spirit of resistance that existed in these camps, particularly at Terezin in North Bohemia. Other documents include the drawings of imprisoned artists, and poems and drawings by the Jewish children from Terezin, of which these are the only relics.

The most impressive single memorial is one bearing the names of the 77,297 unburied victims during the seven-year terror.

Listed alphabetically in black lettering on white walls, with initials in red, the sea of names makes an impact on the visitor which can not be equaled by sculpture or monuments. There is not a family in Czechoslovakia's 15,000 remaining Jews (out of 400,000 before 1938) which would not have a blood relative in that vast tragic scroll of martyrs.

143

THE
VVHOLE
BOOKE OF PSALMES
Faithfully
TRANSLATED *into* ENGLISH
Metre.

Whereunto is prefixed a discourse declaring not only the lawfullnes, but also
the necessity of the heavenly Ordinance
of singing Scripture Psalmes in
the Churches of
God.

Coll. III.

*Let the word of God dwell plenteously in
you, in all wisdome, teaching and exhort-
ing one another in Psalmes, Himnes, and
spirituall Songs, singing to the Lord with
grace in your hearts.*

Iames v.

*If any be afflicted, let him pray, and if
any be merry let him sing psalmes.*

Imprinted
1640

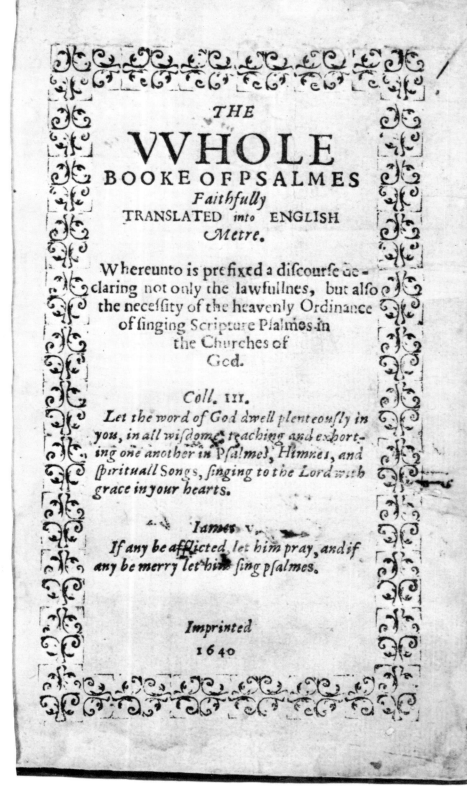

The Bay Psalm Book

1640

The first book printed in America, commonly known as the Bay Psalm Book, was published in 1640. Its exact title reads: *The Whole Booke of Psalmes Faithfully Translated into English Metre. Whereunto is prefixed a discourse declaring not only the lawfullness, but also the necessity of the heavenly Ordinance of singing Scripture Psalmes in the Churches of God . . . Imprinted 1640*. It was translated by a number of New England ministers. The title page mentions no name, place, or printer, but the book is known to have been printed by Stephen Daye at Cambridge, Massachusetts. The press on which the work was done was the gift of friends in Holland. Included in the book are Hebrew words and the Hebrew alphabet. Later editions came to be called *The New England Version of the Psalms*.

In order to appreciate this old book, it is necessary to know that the early New England colonists were a singing people, who used music in all their social gatherings. In their religious services, music based on the Book of Psalms was given first place, since they considered nothing but Scripture suitable for use in religious worship.

The following gives the flavor of the translation, which was a literal rendering of the Hebrew:

> *"The earth Jehova's is*
> *and the fulness of it*:
> *The habitable world and they that thereupon doe sit."*

The book was widely used for many years in New England, and went through several revisions. Only eleven copies of the original edition are now known to exist. It is so rare that even the Library of Congress does not own a copy.

145

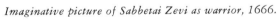

Tikkun Kriah

Early portrait of Shabbetai Zevi

Imaginative picture of Sabbetai Zevi as warrior, 1666.

The Tikkun of Shabbetai Zevi

SEVENTEENTH CENTURY

Shabbetai Zevi (1626-1676), pseudo-Messiah and Kabbalist, was the founder of a sect which rocked the Jewish world in the seventeenth century, and whose tragic aftermath lingered on for scores of years.

Fascinated by mysticism and the *Kabbalah*—and especially by the asceticism and self-denial preached by Rabbi Isaac Luria—the Smyrna-born Shabbetai Zevi imposed on himself a regimen of abstention, mortification, and solitude. Although it left him slightly unbalanced, he began to attract adherents, at a time propitious for an upsurge of mysticism. In 1648-49 hideous pogroms took place in the Ukraine under the Cossack leader Bogdan Chmielnicki. Scores of Jewish communities in southern Russia were destroyed, and tens of thousands of Jewish families were massacred.

To the persecuted Jews their suffering seemed to be the harbinger of the Messiah, whose appearance was predicted for the year 1648 and again for the year 1666. These predictions were made by Christian and Jewish visionaries, kabbalists, and scholars.

In 1648, at the age of twenty-five, Shabbetai Zevi announced himself in Smyrna as the Messiah, whose mission was to restore the Jewish people to Zion and Jerusalem. After he and his followers had been barred from the city, they appeared in Salonika with forged documents and testimonies to his anointing. Banned once again, they moved on to Alexandria and subsequently to Athens, Constantinople, and Jerusalem, before finally settling in Cairo, where Shabbetai Zev consolidated and strengthened his group of followers. In 1663, in anticipation of the fateful year of 1666, he settled in Jerusalem, where through a combination of luck and shrewdness, he continued to attract the superstitious and credulous.

Finally, at the New Year in 1665, Shabbetai Zevi proclaimed himself Messiah at his birthplace in Smyrna. With his consent his followers began to change the Jewish ritual. The movement split many Jewish communities in Europe, Asia, and Africa, engendering hatred, fear, and strife. Prayers composed in his honor were recited on the Sabbath and on Monday and Thursday mornings. Shown here is a *Tikkun,* a collection of prayers, with a drawing of Shabbetai Zevi enthroned by angels and wearing a crown on which is inscribed, "Crown of Zevi." Underneath is a prophetic utterance announcing the coming of the Messiah. The *Tikkun* was printed in Amsterdam in 1666.

Rembrandt's Manasseh ben Israel

SEVENTEENTH CENTURY

Rembrandt, the renowned Dutch painter, was born at Leiden in 1606 (or 1607), and died at Amsterdam in 1669. He was a contemporary and an intimate friend of Rabbi Manasseh ben Israel, whose portrait he painted in 1645. Later Rembrandt did an etching of the same portrait.

Rembrandt's home in Amsterdam was near the Jewish quarter. For his many works on biblical subjects, as well as his portrayals of contemporary Jewish life, he took his models from the ghetto about him. An extensive list of Rembrandt's works of Jewish interest, with some reproductions, may be found in the *Jewish Encyclopedia,* Volume X (pp. 371-375).

Manasseh ben Israel was born at La Rochelle about 1604 and died at Middleburg, Holland, on November 27, 1657. The leading Dutch Jew of his time, he was rabbi of the congregation *N'veh Shalom* ("Dwelling of Peace"), and founded the first Hebrew press in Holland. His published works in Hebrew, Latin, Spanish, Portuguese and English, made him well known in the non-Jewish world, and he carried on a large correspondence with scholars.

Manasseh ben Israel was deeply concerned over the question of the Messiah. He was convinced that the messianic era and the restoration of the Holy Land could not come about until the Jews had been dispersed into every part of the world. He had a particular interest in the readmission of the Jews into England, and actively promoted the idea among the English theologians with whom he corresponded. England was then under the rule of the Puritan leader, Oliver Cromwell, whose thinking was strongly influenced by the Bible. To advance his cause, Manasseh wrote a treatise on the Ten Lost Tribes, contending that their descendants were the American Indians, in further support of his argument for the readmission of Jews into England. Written in Spanish, the book was entitled *Esperanca de Israel* ("Hope of Israel"). A Latin translation, with a prefatory letter addressed to Parliament, was sent to England, where it aroused much comment, both favorable and unfavorable.

In 1555 Manasseh ben Israel arrived in London, where he proceeded to bring out a pamphlet of "Humble Addresses to the Lord Protector." Though he did not succeed in gaining formal permission for the Jews to resettle on English soil, the authorities ruled that there was nothing in the English law to prevent them from doing so.

Manasseh ben Israel
Rembrandt House

239

To His Highnesse Oliuer Lord Protector of The
Comonwelth of England, Scotland and Ireland, & the Dominions thereof

Humbly sheweth   The Humble Petition of The Hebrews at Present
Reziding in this citty of London whose names ar Vnderwritten

That Acknoledging The Manyfold fauours and Protection yor Highnesse hath bin pleased
to graunt Vs in order that wee may with security meete priuatley in our particular houses
to our Deuosions, And being desirous to be fauoured more by yor Highnesse, wee pray with all
Humblenesse yt by the best meanes which may be such Protection may be graunted Vs in
Writting as that wee may therewth meete at our said priuate deuosions in our Particular
houses without feere of Molestation either to our persons famillys or estates, our desires
being to Liue Peaceoly Vnder yor Highnes Gouernement, And being wee ar all mortall wee
alldoe Humbly pray yor Highnesse to graunt Vs Lisence that those which may Dey of our nation
may be buryed in such place out of the cittye as wee shall thinck Conuenient with the Proprietors
leaue in whose Land the place shall be, and soe wee shall as well in our Life tyme, as at our death
be highly fauoured by yor Highnesse for whose Long Life and Prosperity wee shall Continually pray
To the almighty God &c.

Menasseh ben Israel
Dauid Abrabanell
Abraham Israel Carvajal
Abraham Coen Gonsales
Jahacob de Caseres
Abraham Israel de...
Isak Lopes Cillon

Wee doo referr this Petition
to the Consideracion of or Councell.

March ye 24th
1655/6

169

Petition to Oliver Cromwell

1656

One of the basic documents of Anglo-Jewish history is a petition presented to the Lord Protector Oliver Cromwell by a group of Marranos who had fled the Spanish Inquisition and settled in England. In the petition they threw themselves at Cromwell's mercy, requesting permission to congregate for Jewish religious services in their own homes and to have a cemetery outside the city of London. The petition was accepted by Cromwell. He noted the date, March 24, 1655-6 (the calendar was then in a period of transition from old to new style), and wrote in the quaint spelling of the time that he had referred the "peticon" to the "Consideracon of ye Council."

For almost a hundred years scholars searching for the action by the Council and Cromwell were baffled by the absence of a decision. Yet strangely enough Manassah ben Israel had written to Amsterdam some time later asking for a Sepher Torah (Scroll of the Law) to be used by the Jewish community in London. Moreover, negotiations were begun to bring a minister from Hamburg to London. How then can one account for the mystifying absence of a positive response from Cromwell before these negotiations?

In an essay *The Mystery of the Resettlement* by Cecil Roth in *Essays and Portraits in Anglo Jewish History* (Jewish Publication Society, 1962), Dr. Roth points out the key to the mystery. A discovery had been made that the pages containing the minutes for the proceedings in the Book of the Council of State of June 25, 1656, are missing. After a careful calculation, Roth opines that this was the date a favorable decision was reached by the Council; and it was forwarded by Cromwell to Rabbi Manasseh on the following day.

Encouraged by the decision, which must have been quite favorable, the Marranos, now free to practice their religion in the open, decided to find a permanent house of worship instead of using their own homes. A short time later "The First London Synagogue of the Resettlement" was leased in Cree Church and will be seen on page 159.

After a period of 366 years since the Jews had been expelled from England, Jewish public worship was restored and with it the Jewish community in England.

152

The Oldest Jewish Cemetery in the New World

1659

The walled cemetery outside the city of Curaçao, consecrated in 1659, is the oldest Jewish burial ground still in use in the Western Hemisphere. It covers about three acres. More than twenty-five hundred of the headstones are still in good condition; the epitaphs are in Portuguese, Hebrew, Dutch, Spanish, and English.

The oldest legible inscription is on a stone marking the grave of Judith Nunes da Fonesca, who died in January, 1668.

The carving of some of the stones shows great artistic talent. Replicas have been made of a number of the most beautiful, since as a result of exposure to the weather and the acid fumes from a nearby refinery, they might otherwise be totally lost.

For twenty years after its consecration this cemetery was the only one used by the Jewish community of Curaçao. In 1680 another was consecrated, but the old burial place is still in use.

Of special interest to American visitors is the grave of Eliao Hiskiao Touro, who died 3 Ab 5434 (1674). He was the uncle of Isaac de Abraham Touro, whose family founded the Touro Synagogue in Newport, Rhode Island, the oldest synagogue still standing in the United States and one of the country's historic shrines.

Tombstones

Entrance to synagogue
Interior

Portuguese Synagogue of Amsterdam

1675

Foundations for the Portuguese Synagogue of Amsterdam were laid in April 1671. This house of worship became one of the most prestigious in Europe, serving as a model for the Spanish and Portuguese communities of London and the New World.

The synagogue enjoyed the high status of the Portuguese Jewish community in Amsterdam, consisting of Marranos who had fled the Iberian Peninsula in order to return to Judaism. On the whole a wealthy and intellectual group, they had established international connections and were leaders in commerce and world trade.

Construction of the synagogue began with the laying of four cornerstones by four congregants who had made large gifts. Incidentally, one of these was the financial agent of the Portuguese king, who had engaged a "non-believer" to handle his royal affairs.

The response to the purchase of the plot and the building of the synagogue was generous. Even non-Jews, whose sympathies and friendship were aroused by the aristocratic and elegant newcomers, helped in the project.

The service of dedication, which went on for six days, was held early in August 1675. Music was furnished by a choir and orchestra, with Rabbi Isaac da Fonesca Aboab officiating on the first day and his students continuing the ceremonies.

The synagogue measures 125 by 95 feet and seats 1,227 men and 440 women. The women sit in galleries. It consists of three stories; a ground floor, a middle floor, and an attic. The pulpit or *bimah,* as it is commonly known today, is located toward the rear of the hall. The warden's or trustee's bench is at the north wall. The *bimah* and ark are made of valuable wood from Brazil.

The ark, which occupies most of the eastern wall, is crowned with two Tablets of the Law. The interior is illuminated by 1,000 candles.

The design of the synagogue shows the influence of a wooden model of Solomon's Temple, made by a Jew who lived in Amsterdam during the first half of the seventeenth century.

To this day it has remained an historic and architectural landmark in the city of Amsterdam.

Tombstone of the Reverend Gershom Mendes Seixas, 1816

Tablet over the cemetery gateway

Chatham Square Cemetery in downtown New York in use from 1682 to 1831

Oldest Jewish Cemetery in North America

1682

At the corner of Madison and Oliver Streets, bounded by what is now New Bowery, below Chatham Square, is the oldest known burial ground of the Jews of New York. (There had been an older cemetery but its site could not be traced.) When originally purchased "for the Jewish nation in New York" by Joseph Bueno de Mesquita in 1682, it was an irregular quadrangle measuring about 54 by 52 feet; later additional land was acquired. In use from 1682 to 1831, it was controlled by Congregation Shearith Israel, more often known as the Spanish and Portuguese Synagogue (now at Central Park West and 70th Street).

Among the many notables buried here is Gershon Mendes Seixas, the first American-born Jewish minister (b. N.Y.C. January 14, 1745; d. July 2, 1816), who was both a patriot and a religious leader. It was Gershon Mendes Seixas who addressed the letter of welcome to George Washington. When fear of invasion by the British forced him to leave New York, he moved from place to place in Connecticut and in Philadelphia, whose first synagogue he dedicated on September 13, 1782.

Seixas returned to New York in 1784 to continue his services as minister, *hazzan* (cantor), Hebrew teacher, *shohet* (ritual slaughterer) and *mohel* (performer of the circumcision rite). As the representative of the Jewish community he was present at the inauguration of George Washington, first president of the United States. He also served as a trustee of Columbia College, and as a member of the first Board of Regents of New York State, and held other distinguished offices.

A tablet marks the remains of this cemetery, the oldest Jewish landmark in the United States.

Bevis Marks Synagogue, London, England

1702

Established by the Sephardic Jews in 1698, this synagogue, also known as *Shaar ha-Shamayim* ("Gate of Heaven"), is the oldest house of worship in London. The congregation first met in a small building in Cree Church Lane. In 1699 they leased a plot of land in Bevis Marks, at Plough Yard, for construction of a new synagogue. The lease, at a nominal fee, was for sixty-one years, with an option of renewal for another thirty-eight years. Later the acquisition was made permanent. Completed and dedicated in 1702, the building was reconstructed after a fire in 1749.

The design of the interior shows the influence of the Amsterdam Synagogue. In its roof is a beam from a royal ship, presented to the congregation by Queen Anne of England.

For more than a century the Bevis Marks Synagogue served as the religious center for the philanthropic, social, and political activities of English Jewry in behalf of Jews the world over. At one time, although nothing came of the project, its leaders negotiated for acquisition of land in Georgia and Carolina so that their poor brethren might emigrate to begin a new life in the New World. The Jews of Jamaica were constantly in need of assistance from the wardens or trustees of Bevis Marks, to protect their right in the British colony there. So were the Jews of Barbados. Congregation Bevis Marks was called upon to save captive Jews held for ransom by the pirates of Tripoli, and to liberate Jewish prisoners from the Turks. Often they rescued Marrano families and delivered them safely from Portugal. Bevis Marks also furnished religious functionaries to the new synagogues founded by their kin in the New World. However, when it celebrated its bi-centenary in 1901, there were very few descendants of the early leaders left in the congregation.

Bevis Marks boasted among its membership such eminent families as that of Isaac Disraeli, whose son Benjamin, born in 1804, became Prime Minister of England. Isaac broke away from the synagogue and from the Jewish faith because of the rigid discipline of Bevis Marks.

On the other hand, Bevis Marks took deep pride in its most distinguished son, greatest English Jew of the nineteenth century and noblest benefactor of his people, Sir Moses Montefiore. A pious warden of the synagogue, he and his wife, Lady Judith, were the great protectors, philanthropists, and builders of world Jewry. Their memory lives on undimmed.

Interior of synagogue
Entrance

Oldest Synagogue in New World

1732

The synagogue of Congregation Mikve Israel in Curacao, consecrated in the year 1732, is the oldest in the Western Hemisphere still in active use.

Above the entrance is a text in Hebrew (Genesis IX:27) which reads: "May God enlarge Japheth and he shall dwell in the tents of Shem."

Some of the synagogue's furnishings are actually older than the building itself. For thirty years before the present building was constructed they had been used in an earlier structure on the same location. Among these are four massive 24-candle candelabra hung from the ceiling. Made of solid brass, they are copies of those that adorn the famous synagogue of the Portuguese Jewish Congregation at Amsterdam. On the reader's platform stand eight huge candlesticks, also of brass. These too are replicas of those in Amsterdam, and are older than the building.

The Holy Ark with its eighteen *Sefarim*, or Scrolls of the Law, is a masterpiece of richly carved mahogany, standing seventeen feet high and fifteen feet wide. At its top are the two Tablets, also of mahogany, on which are hammered solid silver letters of the Ten Commandments in relief.

All the woodwork of the building is mahogany. The seats for the members and the women's gallery are heavy, dark, and somber. Originally the ceiling and the upper gallery were painted white so as to lessen the gloom of the interior.

One curious traditional feature of the synagogue is the covering of its floor with sand. The original reason for this practice is uncertain. It may have been that the sand was meant to be a symbolic reminder of the days of the Tabernacle during the wanderings of the Israelites through the desert. Or it may have been simply a practical measure to muffle the sound of footsteps on the tiled floor.

Etrog Receptacle

Hanukkah menorah

161

The Synagogue at Newport, Rhode Island

1763

The Touro Synagogue (so named for its first rabbi, Isaac Touro) of Congregation *Yeshuat Israel*, was dedicated on the first day of Hanukkah, 1763 (just two years under two millennia after reconstruction of the Temple at Jerusalem by Judah Maccabee, 165 B. C. E.). The work of the colonial architect Peter Harrison, it is a blend of American colonial style with the traditional Spanish-Portuguese style of the synagogue at Amsterdam and the Bevis Marks synagogue in London. It was placed at an angle, so that the wall containing the Holy Ark would face directly east. Here, in a wooden cupboard, three Torah scrolls written on vellum were kept; one of these had been brought from Amsterdam and was already two hundred years old when the synagogue was dedicated.

The women's gallery runs along three sides of the building; it is supported by twelve columns, representing the Twelve Tribes of Israel. On the north wall is a raised seat for the elders, and just west of the center of the room is the pulpit for the reading of the Law. A small stairway leads directly from the reading desk to a secret passageway in the basement—a relic of the dread days of the Inquisition which the Jews of colonial Newport, most of whom were Marranos, had carried over into the land of freedom. Long ago the tunnel had an exit which is no longer in existence.

Adjacent to the north side of the synagogue is a school building from which there are stairs leading to the women's gallery. In this building is an oven that was used to bake unleavened bread for the Feast of Passover.

In 1946 it was designated by the United States Government as a national historic site—the first Jewish religious shrine in the country to be so distinguished.

Liberty Bell

1776

The Liberty Bell, perhaps the most cherished emblem in all the United States, is treasured by the Jewish people because of the verse from Leviticus XXV:10 inscribed upon it: "Proclaim liberty throughout all the land unto all the inhabitants thereof."

According to popular legend, at two o'clock on July 4, 1776, the door of the State House in Philadelphia opened, and a voice called out that the Declaration of Independence had just been passed. As the word went out, the bellman seized the iron clapper and hurled it forward, to proclaim the motto that encircled the bell.

As is well known, the emblem of liberty is marred by a zigzag fissure extending from the rim into the lettering. At its widest point the crack is nearly three-fourths of an inch across. The lip of the bell is ragged and roughened by the dents of hammer and chisel and from later mutilation. The outer surface of the bell is uneven; it does not look like a finished casting.

In circumference the Liberty Bell measures 12 feet around the lip, 7 feet 6 inches around the crown, and 2 feet 3 inches over the crown. It is 3 inches thick near the lip and $1\frac{1}{4}$ inches thick toward the crown. The length of the clapper is 3 feet 2 inches, and the weight of the whole is 2,000 pounds. The bell cost £60 14s. 5d., and was cast in England at the foundry of Pass and Stow.

To the Hebrew Congregation in Newport
Rhode Island.

Gentlemen

While I receive, with much satisfaction, your Address replete with expressions of affection and esteem; I rejoice in the opportunity of assuring you, that I shall always retain a grateful remembrance of the cordial welcome I experienced in my visit to Newport, from all classes of Citizens.

The reflection on the days of difficulty and danger which are past is rendered the more sweet, from a consciousness that they are succeeded by days of uncommon prosperity and security. If we have wisdom to make the best use of the advantages with which we are now favored, we cannot fail, under the just administration of a good Government, to become a great and a happy people.

The Citizens of the United States of America have a right to applaud themselves for having given to mankind examples of an enlarged and liberal policy: a policy worthy of imitation. All possess alike liberty of conscience and immunities of citizenship. It is now no more that toleration is spoken of, as if it was by the indulgence of one class of people, that another enjoyed the exercise of their inherent natural rights. For happily the

the Government of the United States, which gives to bigotry no sanction, to persecution no assistance requires only that they who live under its protection should demean themselves as good citizens, in giving it on all occasions their effectual support.

It would be inconsistent with the frankness of my character not to avow that I am pleased with your favorable opinion of my administration, and fervent wishes for my felicity. May the children of the Stock of Abraham, who dwell in this land, continue to merit and enjoy the good will of the other Inhabitants; while every one shall sit in safety under his own vine and figtree, and there shall be none to make him afraid. May the father of all mercies scatter light and not darkness in our paths, and make us all in our several vocations useful here, and in his own due time and way everlastingly happy.

G Washington

Washington's Letter to the Hebrew Congregation in Newport, R.I.

1790

When George Washington was elected first President of the United States, the Jewish congregations of New York, Newport, Philadelphia, Charleston, and Savannah sent him letters of congratulation, expressing their loyalty and best wishes. Washington responded in letters which have become classics for their spirit of toleration. The most famous of these; addressed to the Warden of the Hebrew Congregation at Newport, Rhode Island, contains the memorable statement: "For happily the Government of the United States . . . gives to bigotry no sanction, to persecution no assistance." This sentiment has enshrined it in the hearts of Americans, Jews and citizens of all minority groups. Purchased by Morris Morgenstern of New York, the letter is on exhibit at the Jewish Museum in New York City.

Portion of letter to George Washington

Torah headpieces

Pipe lighter

Salt cellars

Receptacle

Craftsmanship of Myer Myers, Silversmith

EIGHTEENTH CENTURY

The first native-born Jew to contribute to American art was Myer Myers (1723-1795). Like his contemporary Paul Revere, he was a gifted silversmith, whose works, signed "M. M." or "Myers," are cherished in the museums, synagogues and churches of New York, Brooklyn, Philadelphia, Boston, St. Louis, and elsewhere.

Myers' parents emigrated from Holland, and his father was given citizenship rights in New Amsterdam, so that when the son grew up he was permitted to become an apprentice to a goldsmith, from whom he learned his trade. After the required term of seven years he opened his own shop. His craftsmanship was regarded highly and his customers were members of the aristocracy in New York. His productions included objects for churches, private homes, and synagogues. His was a long, active career of fifty years. He prospered and bought tracts of land in New Hampshire and Connecticut. Myers was a leader in the general and Jewish communities. He was active against the Tories in the American Revolution. A devoted attendant at the synagogue, he contributed not only to his own congregation, *Shearith Israel*, but also to the erection of Spanish and Portuguese synagogues in Philadelphia and in Newport.

His ancestral faith was fully expressed in the Torah decorations he designed for synagogues in New York, Newport, and Philadelphia. His high professional standing caused him to be elected chairman of the Gold and Silver Society, a rare distinction for a Jew in those early days.

Tomb of Rabbi Nahman of Bratslav

1811

Rabbi Nahman of Bratslav (1772-1811) was a founder of the hassidic movement and the great grandson of Israel Baal-Shem-Tov, founder of Hassidism. From early childhood he absorbed the hassidic doctrine as well as the teachings of the Kabbalah, the study of Jewish mysticism. In 1798-1799 he lived in Tiberias, Palestine, absorbing the Kabbalah and immersing himself in mystic studies.

In 1802 he settled in Bratslav, Ukraine, where his disciple Rabbi Nathan wrote down his teachings and stories. Rabbi Nahman developed the idea of the place of the *tzaddik*, who is the "divine image of the generation," and serves as an "intermediary" between man and God. Rabbi Nahman told his followers many parables and stories in Yiddish, and these were set down by his disciples.

In 1810 he settled in Uman, where he died a year later. His followers did not choose a new rabbi, but remained faithful to his memory.

An *ohel* (tent) or wooden shack was erected on his grave, which his followers visit to this day. They pray and leave *kvitlach*, notes of paper petitioning the help and succor of the sainted rabbi.

In recent years some Bratslav hassidim visited Uman to pray at Rabbi Nahman's grave. They found the cemetery destroyed, and houses built around and over it. But the "ohel" of the rabbi remained intact. Evidently, even the communists respect the memory of the sainted Rabbi Nahman.

תורה נביאים וכתובים

BIBLIA HEBRAICA,

SECUNDUM ULTIMAM EDITIONEM

JOS. ATHIAE,

A

JOHANNE LEUSDEN

DENUO RECOGNITAM,

RECENSITA VARIISQUE NOTIS LATINIS ILLUSTRATA

AB

EVERARDO VAN DER HOOGHT,

V. D. M.

EDITIO PRIMA AMERICANA, SINE PUNCTIS
MASORETHICIS.

TOM. II.

───────

PHILADELPHIÆ:
CURA ET IMPENSIS THOMÆ DOBSON EDITA EX ÆDIBUS LAPIDEIS.
TYPIS GULIELMI FRY.
MDCCCXIV.

The First Hebrew Bible Printed in America

1814

The first American Hebrew Bible is a facsimile of the original edition of the Van der Hooght Bible, published in Amsterdam in 1705. The idea was originally conceived in 1812 by a Mr. Howitz, who, supported in the undertaking by a number of clergymen, succeeded in obtaining a large number of subscriptions. Early in 1813 Mr. Howitz transferred publication rights, along with the list of subscriptions, to Thomas Dobson of Philadelphia. 1n 1814 the Van de Hooght edition was finally chosen. Published in Philadelphia by Thomas Dobson, it immediately gained popular recognition.

The Bible is in two volumes and contains the Latin introduction to the Van der Hooght edition, along with ten endorsements by Christian authorities. Marginal notes in Latin give brief synopses of the various passages.

שמע ישראל יי אלהינו יי אחד

ARARAT.
A City of Refuge for the Jews.
Founded by Mordecai Manuel Noah in the Month Tizri 5586 Septr. 1825 & in the 50th year of American Independence

New York Sep 27 1824

Dear Sir

Will you have the kindness to inform me whether the Survey of Grand Island has been completed and what the land has been valued at — I am also desirous of learning at what period you will fix for the Sale of the same —

Very respectfully yours

M. M. Noah

Letter from Noah

Major Noah's Ararat

1825

In the Buffalo Historical Society lies a stone inscribed in Hebrew with the *Shema Yisrael,* the watchword of every Jew, and in English as follows:

> ARARAT
> A City of Refuge for the Jews
> Founded by MORDECAI MANUEL NOAH
> for the month of Tizri Sept. 1825 &
> in the Fiftieth Year of American Independence

This was the cornerstone to be laid for a Jewish state by one of the most flamboyant and versatile American Jews, Mordecai Manuel Noah. He was United States consul, editor of influential newspapers, sheriff of New York City, counselor-at-law, judge, dramatist, founder of New York University, and self-styled "Governor and Judge of Israel."

The ceremony of laying the cornerstone took place in an Episcopal church at Buffalo on Sunday morning, September 15, 1825, in the midst of a salvo fired from a cannon. It began with a parade led by Mordecai Noah, continued with a religious service in which selections from the Prophets and the Psalms were read in English and Hebrew, and ended with a grandiose "Proclamation to the Jews."

Ararat, whose name was that of the mountain on which Noah's ark rested after the flood, was to be established on Grand Island in the Niagara River, Erie County, New York State—an area of some 50 square miles.

Nothing came of this utopian dream, but the eccentric Noah has been accorded a place of honor in the Jewish Hall of Fame, and has become the subject of Jewish fiction and drama, as the first dreamer of founding a Jewish state, generations before Theodor Herzl made Zionism a political reality.

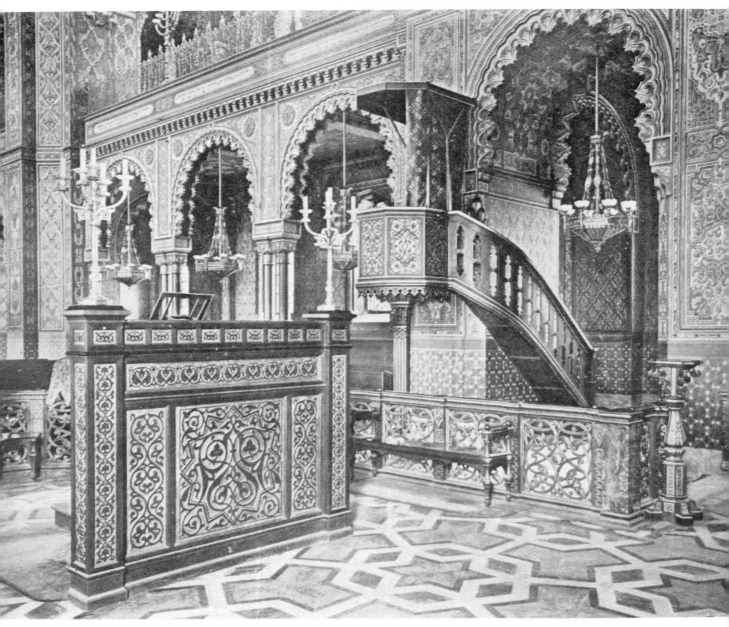

Pulpit and Ark

176

The Florentine Synagogue

1882

The monumental Sephardic synagogue at 4 Via L.C. Farini in Florence, Italy, is one of the most beautiful in Europe. The building, made possible by a former president of the *kehillah* (community), David Levi, was begun in 1874 and completed in 1882, and is in pure Moorish style. The interior is decorated with frescoes, and the sanctuary with rich Venetian mosaics. During World War II the Nazis and Fascists used the synagogue as a medical warehouse, and partially destroyed it when they were forced to retreat. It was rebuilt after the war with the help of the Italian government, the Joint Distribution Committee, and the Claims Conference, and today it is one of the historical monuments of Florence.

In the first thirty years of this century, Florence was considered the center of Italian Jewry. Here the Italian Rabbinical College had its home, before its removal to Rome; here again, the Israel Publishing House was born. Today Florence ranks as the third largest Jewish community in Italy, after Rome and Milan.

Interior

Exterior

ר"ע מברטנורה   כלים פרק א   תוספות יום טוב   א   תוספות ראשון לציון

סדר טהרות · בענין הטהרות והפכם · הרמב"ם :

מסכת כלים התחיל במסכת כלים ועניינו שהוא כולל עקרי הטומאות ולזכור מה שהוא מקבל טומאה ושאינו מקבל טומאה
כי כשיזכר לנו מה שהוא מקבל טומאה נדע כל הדברים שהם מקבלים טומאה ושאינם מקבלים · הרמב"ם ·

מסכת כלים

פרק א אבות הטומאות השרץ · שמנה שרצים הכתובים
בפרשת ויהי ביום השמיני החלד והעכבר
וכו' · והן אבות הטומאות · לטמא אדם וכלים הנוגעים בהם
במותם · אבל האברים אין להם
שעור · אפילו פחות מכעדשה
מן השרץ · מטמאין · ודוקא כשהוא
לח השרץ מטמא ואינו מטמא
יבש · דכתיב (ויקרא י"א) וכל
אשר יפול עליו מהם במותם ·
כעין מותם · ושכבת זרע · דוקא
שכבת זרע דישראל · וגדול ·

וכן שכבת זרע של קטן נמי לא מטמא · דכתיב (שם ט"ו)
ואיש כי תצא ממנו שכבת זרע · איש · ולא קטן פחות מבן
ט' שנים ויום אחד דאין ביאתו ביאה · ושיעורה לרואה
במשהו אפילו כענין מרדל · ולמגע בכעדשה · ודוקא ש"ז למה
מטמאה · דכתיב שכבת זרע · פרט למי שהוא להזריע · ומדלא קחשיב
תנא דידן בעל קרי בהדי אבות הטומאות ש"מ דאינו אלא
ראשון לטומאה והכי תנן בסוף מסכת זבים · בעל קרי כמגע
שרץ דלא הוי אלא ראשון : וטמא מת · אדם שנטמא במת ·
אבל כלים שנטמאו במת הן כמת עצמו · והנוגע בהן נעשה אב
הטומאה · וכלים שנגעו באדם · שנטמא במת. או באדם
שנגע בכלים שנגעו במת · הוו אב הטומאה · ושמאים טומאת
שבעה כאדם · כדתנן פ"ק דאהלות · אבל כלי מרם וכלים
ומשקים שנגעו במת אין נעשים אב הטומאה ודוקא ישראל
נעשה אב הטומאה כשנגע במת · וכן נפל שכול בן מ' אינו
מקבל טומאה אם נגע במת · והמצורע בימי ספרו · מצורע
שהחלם בתוך ימי הנגעים ונתרפא · והוכשר לצפורים ועץ
ארז ואזוב ושני תולעת · ותגלחת · ויולא מחוץ לאהלו שבעת
ימים · ובשמיני מביא קרבנותיו · ואותם ז' ימים קרויין ימי
ספרו · ומטמא אדם · דנאמר כבוס בגדים בימי חלוטו
ונאמר כבוס בגדים בימי ספרו · מה להלן מטמא אדם אף
כאן מטמא אדם · ומי חטאת שאין בהם כדי הזיה · מטמא
במגע · ואם יש בהן כדי היה היה מטמא אף במשא · לטמא
אדם לטמא בגדים · דכתיב (במדבר י"ט) ומזה מי הנדה
יכבס בגדיו · והנוגע במי הנדה יטמא עד הערב · ורבותינו

במשנה י"א וסם מאריך בזה בס"ד · וטמא מת · כתב הר"ב ומ"ש הר"ב · אינו מקבל טומאה כו' · וכן נפל שכול בן מ' כו' · בפ"צ דב"ב (דף כ') אבל בר קיימא אפילו של יום אחד מיטמא
מטמא דגמ' · ברפ"ק דנזיר ומ"ש הר"ב · לטמא לטמא בפ"ק דב"ב · בסם אמרו בגמ' למדו שהמים טהור · בפ"ק דנדה (דף פ') אמרו בגמ' דקרא לאו במזה כו' · אלא בנוגאל כו'
במטמא מת · כדתנן בפ"ה דנדה דנדה משנה ג' · ומי חטאת · טייז מעטא · פי"א דפרה : שאין בהם כדי היה · כתב
הר"ב דכתיב ומזה וגו' · ורבותינו בגמ' · וכחבו התום' ונ"מ ומעליה לאפוקי קרא ממשמעותיה וי"ל מדכתיב (במדבר י"ט) והזה הטהור על הטמא משמע שהוא טהור
לעולם · ואף על גב דדרשינן מיניה · הטהור מכלל שהוא טמא לימד על טבול יום שטהור כמ"ש במשנה ז' פרק ג' דפרה
חלקי

[ח"א] אלף א

The Vilna Shas (Talmud)

1897

In 1897 an edition of the Talmud with all important commentaries, based on manuscripts, among others, in the libraries of Paris, the Vatican, the Universities of Cambridge and Oxford, was published in Vilna by the House of the Widow and Brothers Romm. This, the *Vilna Shas*, became the standard edition; it has since been reprinted many times and in many places, including the United States. In an appendix to the final volume the chief editor at the Romm publishing house, Shrage Feivish Feygenson, told in detail how the edition had been planned and executed. The House of Romm, the most famous Jewish press in Russia, employed eminent Jewish scholars as editors, typesetters and proofreaders. It also brought out various editions of the Bible, the prayerbooks, and the Midrash, as well as secular literature in both Hebrew and Yiddish; but its fame in Jewish history rests on its edition of the Talmud.

The establishment of the publishing house by Baruch ben Joseph Romm, in 1789, was an important event in the development of Vilna as a center of Jewish culture. Originally the press was set up in Grodno, but a year later its founder moved it to Vilna. In 1858 it became the property of the widow Deborah Romm, who had married a descendant, and her two brothers-in-law. An energetic and capable woman, she became head of the firm in 1863, and under her leadership it became known throughout the Jewish world.

Deborah Romm died in 1902, and the heirs sold the firm in 1910 to the family of Baron Horace Ginzberg of St. Petersburg. Later it was acquired by Jewish entrepreneurs. During the First World War and the years that followed, the firm declined, owing to the disappearance of the great Russian Jewish market and to the competition of Jewish publishing houses in Warsaw, Lvov, Lublin, and Petrikow. Nevertheless it continued to reprint from its old plates, and published some new books as well, up until the Soviet occupation of Vilna in 1940. Then it was confiscated by the government for its own purposes. In June 1941 the Germans occupied the city, and removed some of the machinery from the Press. In the struggle against the Nazis, Jewish partisan fighters melted down some of the machinery into bullets.

The famous Romm Press is no more, although its world renowned Talmud is still studied in reprint editions.

Commission d. Zionisten-Congresses
Wien,
II., Rembrandtstr. 11.

אדון נכבד!

ביום א׳ ב׳ ו-ג׳ אלול ש״ז יתאספו חו״צ בכל הארצות לקונגרס-הציוני
בבזל (בשוויץ). והיום ההוא, שבו יתאחדו אחינו המפוזרים בדעה אחת,
יהיה יום נצחון לתחית לאומנו. האספה בבאזל תהיה התחלת תקופה
חדשה בהתפתחות תנועתנו.

שם יספרו לנו אחינו מכל פנות הארץ ע״ד מצבם ומגמותיהם, שם יתברר
מה התנועה הציונית דורשת ממעריציה. שם תתרכז ותתאחד פעילתנו,
שהיתה קרועה לכמה גזרים, ע״י הנהגה כוללת לכל סניפי העבודה. שם
תראינה עינינו קבוץ-גליות, שיאחד כל הכחות לפעולה אחת, גדולה וכבירה.
הקונגרס ישאף למטרות קרובות ואפשריות. כל הידיעות האחרות
על אדתיו קלוטות מן האויר. כל מעשי הקונגרס יהיו בפרסום גמור.
שמוחיו והחלטותיו לא תהיה שום התנגדות לחוקי איזו ארץ ולחובותיע
האזרחים. ביהוד אנחנו ערבים בזה, שכל מעשי האספה יהיו באופן
מקובל ומרוצה לחו״צ ברוסיא ולממשלתם הרוממה.

בזה נבקש או..ך,אדון נכבד,ואת הכריך שבחונך,שתואילו לבא לבזל
ולהשתתף באספתנו. הקונגרס הראשון שלנו הוא התל שהכל פונים אליו.
אוהבים ואויבים מחכים לו בעינים כלות.ולכן עליו להראות לעלבי חפצנו
ברור ויכלתנו גדולה. אם לא ימלא הקונגרס את תפקידו, אז תבא עי״כ נסיגה
לאחור בתנועתנו לזמן רב. והכל תלוי רק בהשתתפות מרובה של
אחינו ברוסיא, ששם רוב מניננו.

אנו מקוים, שתדעו את חובתכם ותבאו לאספתנו. באספה אפשר יהיה
לדבר עברית. בבאזל יש אכסניא כשרה.
דבר בואך מהר נא להודיענו עפ״י הכתבת הנ״ל.

בשם „הועד להכנת הקונגרס הציוני״:

Dr. Marcus Ehrenpreis
המזכיר

Dr. Theodor Herzl
ראש-הועד

Buchdruckerei Max Bruck, Diakovar. 2369.—97.

Invitation to the First Zionist Congress

1897

Political Zionism was born at the First Zionist Congress in Basel, Switzerland on August 29-31, 1897. Shown here is the invitation to the Congress, in Hebrew, signed by Dr. Theodor Herzl, its founder, and Dr. Marcus Ehrenpreis, secretary.

On September 3, 1897, Herzl wrote in his diary: "If I were to subsume the Basel Congress in one word—which I shall not do openly—it would be this: at Basel I founded the Jewish State.

"If I were to say this today, I would be met by universal laughter. In five years, perhaps, and certainly in fifty,* everyone will see it. The State is already founded, in essence, in the will of the people to the State; yes, even in the will of one individual, if he is powerful enough. The territory is only the concrete manifestation; and even where it possesses a territory, the State is always something abstract.

"In Basel I created this thing which is abstract and which is therefore invisible to the great majority of people. Actually, with infinitesimal means, I gradually infused into the people the mood of the State and inspired them with the feeling that they were the National Assembly.

"Months ago, I had already decided that one of my methods would be to demand that delegates come to the opening in frockcoats and white cravats. The results were splendid. Festive dress makes most people stiff. Out of this stiffness came a moderation which they would perhaps not have exercised in light summer or travel clothes, and I spared nothing to heighten the mood of solemnity.

"And Congress was splendid. Once, while Nordau was in the chair, I went to the back of the hall. The long green table on the platform, the raised seats of the president, the green-draped tribune, the stenographers' and journalists' table made so powerful an impression on me that I went out quickly, in order not to be overcome."

The Congress was attended by 204 delegates from most of the countries of Europe, and also the United States, Algiers, and Palestine. It was indeed the first national Jewish assembly since the dispersion in 70 C.E.

* Actually it took 51 years

obverse

reverse

Medal struck in honor of Zionist Congress

Handwritten sonnet by Emma Lazarus

Emma Lazarus

Tablet on Statue of Liberty

The New Colossus
(Plaque on the Statue of Liberty)

1903

"Give me your tired, your poor,
Your huddled masses yearning to breathe free,
The wretched refuse of your teeming shore,
Send these, the homeless tempest-tost to me,
I lift my lamp beside the golden door!"

These are the last lines of a sonnet inscribed on a plaque at the base of the Statue of Liberty, "Mother of Exiles." It was written by Emma Lazarus as a contribution toward raising a fund to build a pedestal for the statue which has been presented by France to the United States in 1883. The plaque was affixed to the pedestal in 1903.

The poetess Emma Lazarus (b. New York 1849; d. 1887) came of a well-to-do Sephardic Jewish family. A gifted and precocious child, she began writing poetry at the age of fourteen. She was influenced by Ralph Waldo Emerson and by Edmund Clarence Stedman, both of whom encouraged her writing. As a result of her study of Jewish history and literature and her personal acquaintance with the refugees who began coming to the New World after the Russian pogroms in 1881, she was caught up in the Jewish problem. She not only wrote passionately but worked as an agitator and fundraiser on behalf of her people. She became internationally famous, and her friends included such men of letters as Robert Browning, Henry George, William James, and Thomas Henry Huxley. Her published works comprise lyric and dramatic poems, essays, and translations.

She learned Hebrew so that she might be able to translate the poems of such writers of medieval days as Judah Halevi and Ibn Gabirol, among others. Her magazine articles identify her as an avowed Zionist, in a period before the advent of Theodor Herzl. But above all she is immortalized by the sonnet affixed to the pedestal of the Statue of Liberty standing at the gateway to the New World, through which millions of immigrants have passed.

Einstein's Theory of Special Relativity

1913

In 1905, when Albert Einstein began his major research effort in electromagnetic theory, the world of physics was confronted with severe difficulties in understanding the basic principles underlying the phenomena of electricity and magnetism. The theories current at that time supposed the existence of a medium called "the ether" which was responsible for carrying light waves, or electromagnetic disturbances, in much the same way as air carries sound waves. However, experiments carried out by A. A. Michelson and E. W. Morley in the 1880's did not seem to allow for the existence of such an ether. Einstein realized that electromagnetic phenomena possessed no property corresponding to the idea of absolute rest which the ether theories implied. He very carefully built a consistent theory based on the following two assumptions:

1. The Principle of Relativity—
   the laws of physics must be the same in any two frames of reference which are not accelerating with respect to each other.

2. The Principle of the Constancy of the Velocity of Light—
   the velocity of light is the same in all such frames of reference.

These principles lead to a variety of novel and seemingly paradoxical effects, such as the contraction of bodies traveling at high speeds, the apparent increase in the mass of such bodies, and changes in the length of time intervals measured by rapidly moving clocks. The existence of these effects has been verified in modern experiments. The theory which emerged from these two assumptions has been of the most fundamental importance in the subsequent development of physics. It has been of special significance in understanding the structure of nuclei, the production of nuclear energy, and the properties of the fundamental particles of physics.

Also in the year 1905, Einstein made major contributions to the understanding of the molecular structure of matter through his theory of Brownian motion, and helped pave the way for the future quantum theory by studying the quantum behavior of light in the

184

photoelectric effect. He devoted much of his subsequent scientific career to work on the general theory of relativity, which deals with the nature of gravitational forces, and to investigations on a unified theory of fields. For his work on the photoelectric effect, Einstein was awarded the Nobel prize in 1921.

Einstein is generally regarded as the greatest theoretical physicist of this age, and as a scientist equal in intellect to Isaac Newton.

Page from Einstein's General Theory of Relativity at the Hebrew University

DOCUMENT 1.
The Balfour Declaration.

Foreign Office,
November 2nd, 1917.

Dear Lord Rothschild,

I have much pleasure in conveying to you, on behalf of His Majesty's Government, the following declaration of sympathy with Jewish Zionist aspirations which has been submitted to, and approved by, the Cabinet.

"His Majesty's Government view with favour the establishment in Palestine of a national home for the Jewish people, and will use their best endeavours to facilitate the achievement of this object, it being clearly understood that nothing shall be done which may prejudice the civil and religious rights of existing non-Jewish communities in Palestine, or the rights and political status enjoyed by Jews in any other country"

I should be grateful if you would bring this declaration to the knowledge of the Zionist Federation.

Y. in
Arthur James Balfour

Balfour Declaration

1917

The declaration of the British government signed by Mr. Arthur Balfour (1848-1930), then Foreign Secretary and later Lord Balfour, favoring establishment of a Jewish national home in Palestine, was issued on November 2, 1917.

The Declaration, sent in the form of a letter to Lord Walter Rothschild of England, who had been won over to the Zionist cause, was the culmination of the organized campaign begun by Theodor Herzl on establishment of the World Zionist Movement in 1897.

The principles of the Balfour Declaration became the basis for the Palestine Mandate and were ratified by the Council of the League of Nations, with Great Britain designated as the mandatory government.

The exact way in which the Declaration was to be interpreted became the subject of fierce debates. The Jewish people took the position that it was a promise to reconstitute their National Home in Palestine. Since the Arabs rejected the whole concept of a Jewish National Home, a deep hostility developed which led to riots, warfare, and bloodshed, until ultimately the Jewish State was founded in 1948.

Balfour Day, November 2, has become a national holiday in the Jewish calendar, and is observed by Zionists throughout the world.

The Herzl Room at Jerusalem

CA. 1920

At the headquarters of the Keren Kayemeth Le'Yisrael (Jewish National Fund) in Jerusalem, the contents of Theodor Herzl's study in Vienna have been preserved in a room that is almost an exact replica of the original. They include not only his furniture and books but many personal mementos, placed as nearly as possible as they were during the great Zionist leader's lifetime. Among them are portraits of his parents; a cork helmet he wore on his journey to Palestine in 1898; the decorations received from the Sultan of Turkey during his extended negotiations with that ruler in 1901; the passport he took with him to Russia after the pogroms in 1903; and the Scroll of the Torah presented to him by the Jewish community of Vilna on his return from the same journey. An even more stirring memento is a small table which was originally part of the furnishings of a room in Paris. On this table during the trial of Alfred Dreyfus, which he witnessed as a correspondent for a Viennese newspaper, Herzl made the notes that led to his historic formulation of the Zionist program.

After Herzl's death in 1904, David Wolffsohn of Cologne, who succeeded him as president of the Zionist Organization, took charge of his friend's possessions. Later they passed into the keeping of Mr. and Mrs. A. L. Leszynsky in Berlin, and from there to the room in Jerusalem where they may be seen today.

Herzl's tombstone in Jerusalem.

Relics of Russian Jewry

At the turn of this century about five million Jews lived in Russia—including Poland. Despite forcible conversions, occupational and geographical restrictions and pogroms, Russian-Polish Jewry was the most creative dynamic center of modern times. Hasidism, modern Hebrew and Yiddish Literature, the Zionist movement, the Jewish labor movement, the Yiddish and Hebrew Theatre and other movements, were born and flowered there, and made lasting contributions to Jewish life. Biblical and Talmudic scholarship flourished. Heroically they persevered, created and preserved and made significant contributions to Jewish life and culture. It was their heritage that made possible the rebirth of Israel and the rich Jewish communal life in the United States, the American continent and other new world centers.

But, the Communist Revolution in 1917 spelled the doom of the religious, spiritual and cultural life of Russian Jewry. Repressive measures have denationalized and practically extinguished this great center. Since 1920 no Hebrew Bibles and but a limited edition of Prayer Books have been printed. Jews may not circumcize their male children, produce Tefilin (phylacteries), manufacture Tallitot (prayer shawls) or other religious articles. Synagogue services are under close surveillance. An unrelenting, virulent campaign is waged against the State of Israel. Some three million Jews—the second largest world Jewish population center—are effectively and consistently isolated from their brethren. Emigration is severely restricted. Assimilation, loss of identity, are rife. We are eyewitness to the tragic extinction of Russian Jewry.

Despite these unconscionable measures, thousands of Jewish young people gather on Simhat Torah outside the very few synagogues and dance and sing to express the mystique of their deep-rooted identity with their people and faith.

Shown here are the synagogues of Leningrad (1893), Moscow (1891), and relics of the famous Rabbi Moses Ben Israel Isserless (ReMA) in Cracow (b. 1520; d. 1572), a renowned Talmudist, prominent figure in the Council of Four Lands (see p. 130-131) and the great teacher of his generation. Regarded as a saint and sage by

Polish Jewry they said of him "From Moses (Maimonides) to Moses (Isserless) there arose none like Moses."

The flower of Jewish life in Russia, Poland, Lithuania, is no more. Precious memories remain. May we live to see the reunion of our brethren with the world Jewish community.

Leningrad Synagogue

Remu Synagogue, Cracow

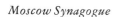

Moscow Synagogue

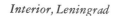

Interior, Leningrad

Memorial of the Warsaw Ghetto Uprising

1948

At the outbreak of World War II there were approximately 370,000 Jews in Warsaw. Within one year, as thousands of refugees crowded into the Polish capital, their number increased to some 433,000. After the German army entered Warsaw on September 29, 1939, the Jewish population lived in constant terror. Walls were erected around the Jewish district, and freedom of movement was severely restricted. On October 16, 1940, the Jewish ghetto was established and all the 140,000 Jews (approximately) who lived outside were forced to move in. Factories, businesses, and workshops outside the ghetto were looted or confiscated by the Germans.

After herding the Jews together the Germans began the campaign to exterminate them. The evacuation of the ghetto was ordered on July 22, 1942, and went on at the average rate of 4,350 daily. By September 21, 1942 the deportation of Warsaw Jews to extermination camps was all but complete.

At midnight April 14, 1943, the first seder night of Passover, the signal was given for a general uprising in the ghetto. Every able-bodied man and woman was given weapons that had been smuggled in. In the morning, the banners of revolt were hung out, the blue and white flag fluttering side by side with the Polish flag.

Warsaw Memo

The heroic struggle raged for six weeks. On the forty-second day of the uprising, one four-story building remained standing in the midst of the ghetto; over it the blue and white flag still waved proudly. Floor by floor, through eight hours of fierce fighting, the Germans captured the last stronghold of Jewish resistance. The next morning they announced in triumph that the ghetto of Warsaw no longer existed. For this "victory" thousands of German soldiers paid with their lives. The martyrs of the ghetto lived with dignity, and died with honor. They had not fought for their own lives, since they knew in advance what their fate would be.

In 1948, a monument was erected on the ruins of the Warsaw ghetto, in commemoration of the Jewish will to survive against impossible odds. The monument's designer was Nathan Rapoport, a Polish-born Jew, who said of his work: "I had to bear in mind not only my responsibility as an artist, but also my responsibility as a Jew. The monument had to express more than my own feelings and emotions; it had to express the feelings and emotions of the Jewish people."

Memorial in Buenos Aires

Ghetto Hero and Martyr
Mordecai Anielewicz

Har Zion

Most revered and sacred of Jerusalem's sites is Mt. Zion. It was the first place inhabited in Jerusalem by King David, and also the last to hold out against Titus and the Roman conquerors of the city. Here King David lived and ruled. Here for 1,000 years, from its heights, ruled the Davidic dynasty. While there is doubt that the alleged tomb of King David on Mount Zion is authentic, the tradition is that King David lies buried there.

A few chapters in the Second Book of Chronicles end by stating the burial of the Davidic kings in the "City of David" or the "Sepulchres of the descendants of David." The famous medieval traveler, Benjamin of Tudela, mentions Mount Zion as the place where King David is buried. In the 12th century a royal tomb was discovered there which was identified as King David's.

Many legends surround the Tomb. They have fed the imagination and folklore particularly of the Jews in Islamic lands. On Shavuot thousands of Jews from all the world and particularly from Mediterranean and Moslem countries visit Mount Zion and King David's Tomb where they celebrate, light candles, pray and sing hymns of praise. On Israel Independence Day the scene is repeated. Twenty-two crowns, symbolizing the twenty-two rulers of the Davidic dynasty, are placed over the Tomb.

Because of its role in Jewish life and tradition, Mount Zion has also become a center of memorializing other events of historical significance. One chamber is devoted to the theme of the *Ingathering of the Exiles*. It contains historical mementos like a famous flag with symbolic inscriptions, a shofar from a concentration camp, a scroll with a memorial prayer for those who lost their lives in valiant attempts to escape to the Land of Israel, and similar objects.

An impressive sanctuary is the Chamber of the Holocaust. Here are stored the Scrolls of the Torah which were desecrated by the Nazis. Exhibited are shoes, drums, and other objects, made of Torah parchments. Here scribes are engaged to repair and reassemble parts of scrolls in order to prepare renewed *Sifre Torah* which would be fit for synagogue use. These are distributed to synagogues in Israel.

In another part of the chamber are urns of ashes of our brethren who were cremated in the death chambers of Europe.

As one ascends the mountain he is greeted by appropriate signs on which are inscribed psalms interspersed at various points. Thus at the entrance the visitor is greeted with Psalm XXIV, beginning with "Who shall ascend into the mountain of the Lord?" And at the entrance to King David's Tomb, Psalm XV, beginning "Who shall dwell in Thy tabernacle?"

First Stamps of the State of Israel

1948

The British mandate over Israel ended May 15, 1948, on the Sabbath, the day of rest. On Sunday, May 16, the first stamps were already on sale at the windows of postoffices of the infant state. These stamps were printed in Israel and not in another country (as have those of many newly founded small states). The stamps were printed before the State was named (there was a discussion whether it should be called Zion, Judah, Israel)—hence the imprint of the neutral phrase *Doar Ivri,* or "Hebrew Post." Nor had the names of the coinage been fixed—hence the blank cyphers 3, 5, 10, and on.

The stamps carried imprints of Hebrew coins from the days of the Second Temple (66-70 C.E.) and the Bar Kokhba Revolt (132-135 C.E.). The artist was Otto Wallish of Tel Aviv, who in designing these coins related them to the days, nineteen hundred years before, when the land of Israel had been an independent commonwealth.

The stamps imprinted with 20 (blue), 250 (dark green), 500 (brown on yellow), and 1000 (blue on blue tinted paper), bear the design of the silver shekel of the first revolt against Rome in 70 C. E. On one side appears likeness of the Temple goblet (similar

דאר עברי

to that on the Arch of Titus), with the ancient Hebrew inscription that had appeared on the shekel; on the other side is a cluster of three pomegranates around which is inscribed *"Jerusalem the Holy"* also in ancient Hebrew script. On the stamps imprinted 5 (green) and 10 (magenta), appear coins minted during the Years II and III of the first Hebrew revolt. On the former is impressed a grape vine; around it the words "Freedom of Zion," on the latter an ancient pitcher and around it "Year Three."

On the 50 stamp (brown) appears a coin from the days of Bar Kokhba rebellion (the second revolt). On it are a *lulav* and *ethrog* (palm branch and citron) and around it the words *"Year One of the Liberation* (or redemption) *of Israel."* A similar inscription appears on the 15 stamp, in whose center is a cluster of grapes.

On the stamp marked 3 (orange) is a replica of the half-shekel of bronze from the fourth year of the first revolt. On it appears a palm tree of seven branches, two clusters of dates, and two baskets filled with fruit, quite possibly to represent the First Fruit offerings to the Temple. The inscription reads, "For the Liberation (or redemption) of Israel." That the palm tree which appears on the Hebrew coins (unlike the palm on non-Hebraic coins), shows seven branches, is due to the special significance of the number seven in Jewish tradition.

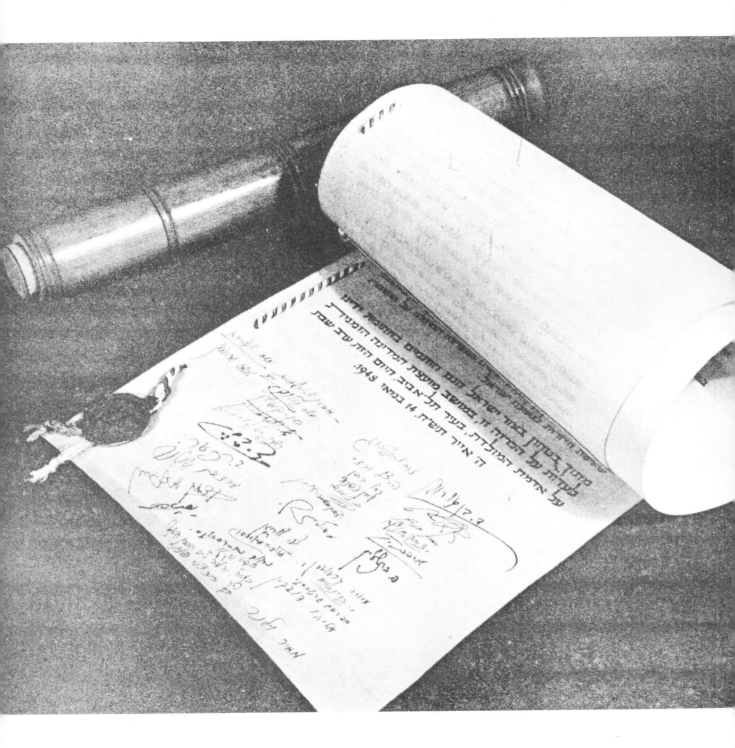

Declaration of Israel Independence

1949

The date was Erev Shabbat, Iyar 5, 5708—Friday, May 14, 1949. The hour was 10:15 A.M.

To the melancholy tune of the "Minstrel Boy" played on a bagpipe, General Alan Cunningham, British High Commissioner for Palestine, stepped aboàrd an English naval launch at Haifa. The thirty-year-old British mandate over Eretz Yisrael was at long last ended. After 1878 years the DAY had finally come . . .

That same day, a few minutes before 4:00 P.M., a historic scene was enacted at the Tel Aviv Museum. Under the tense and watchful eyes of the *Haganah,* the Jewish Self-Defense, thirteen men sat down at a long table. Around them four hundred people, standing under the blue-white flags, began to sing *Hatikvah.* White-haired David Ben-Gurion, first Prime Minister of the state about to be born, arose and read the Proclamation of Independence. As his words rang out to the world, Jews everywhere paraded with blue and white streamers and flags and danced in the streets.

In Washington, amid weeping and cheering, the blue-white flag with the Star of David was hoisted in front of the Jewish Agency building, and a short time later President Harry S. Truman issued the announcement: "The United States Government recognizes the Provisional Government as the *de facto* authority of the new State of Israel." Almost simultaneously the Union of Soviet Socialist Republics also recognized and welcomed the new State into the Family of Nations.

The beginning of the Proclamation of the State of Israel reads: "The Land of Israel was the birthplace of the Jewish people. Here their spiritual, religious, and national identity was formed. Here they achieved independence and created a culture of national and universal significance. Here they wrote and gave the Bible to the world."

The Israel Proclamation of Independence and the signatures are reproduced herewith.

Eternal Light

Memorial in Salonika

200

Yad Vashem

(Martyrs' and Heroes' Remembrance Authority)

1953

On August 19, 1953 the Knesset (Parliament) of Israel passed an act establishing a Memorial Museum, Institute, and Shrine, whose aims were: 1) to preserve the memory of the six million Jewish martyrs who perished at the hands of the Germans and their collaborators during the tragic Nazi period; 2) to collect, examine, and publish all available documents of the Holocaust; 3) to bring home to the world the lessons of this unequaled tragedy so that it might never be experienced again.

Yad Vashem is built on Har Ha-Zikaron—the Mountain of Remembrance—in Jerusalem. A light burning over the Tomb of the Unknown Ashes is frequently rekindled symbolically by survivors of the communities that had been destroyed.

At the Yad Vashem are archives of the Holocaust, accounts by eye witnesses, books, names of those who were wiped out and other historical details, which are constantly being gathered so that the memory of this fearful experience may never be forgotten. It publishes annual studies, periodic bulletins, and other materials related to the tragedy.

To educate the young generation, Yad Vashem also publishes handbooks, anthologies, pictorial and graphic material, and arranges for exhibits throughout the world. It keeps in touch with appropriate world agencies, and maintains contact with national and international legislative bodies whose aim is to prevent a repetition of such unspeakable bestiality of man to man.

Yad Vashem building

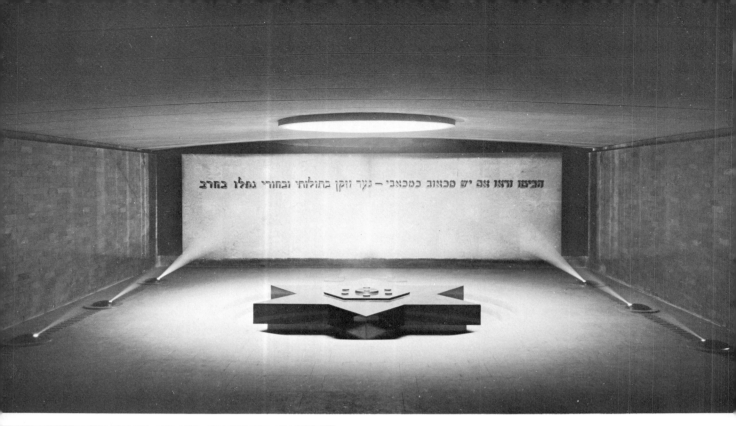

הביטו וראו אם יש מכאוב כמכאבי – נער זקן בתולותי ובחורי נפלו בחרב

Interior and Eternal Light

וכל את אשר עשר יד אדם לאלהים...
...עץ ואבן אשר לא יראון ולא ישמעון
...ולא יאכלון ולא יריחון

DEVANT LE MARTYR JUIF INCONNU
INCLINE TON RESPECT TA PIETE POUR TOUS LES MARTYRS
CHEMINE EN PENSEE AVEC EUX LE LONG DE LEUR VOIE
DOULOUREUSE ELLE TE CONDUIRA AU PLUS HAUT SOMMET
DE JUSTICE ET DE VERITE

Memorial of the Unknown
Jewish Martyr in Paris

1956

At 17 Rue Geoffroy-L'Asnier, in the fourth arondissement near the Jewish quarter and the Paris City Hall (Hotel de Ville) is a four-story building whose front is a blank stone wall. On it is inscribed in Hebrew: *"Remember what the Amalek of our time did to you. He cut off the lives of six million Jewish souls, men, women and children—helpless, defenseless."* Below is inscribed in French: *"Bow your head in reverence to the Unknown Jewish Martyr. It is the reverence you pay to all martyrs. Proceed in your thoughts along their road of martyrdom. It will lead you to the pinnacle of justice and truth."*

Directly above the doors is a Shield of David; inscribed on each side, in Hebrew and in Yiddish, is the word *Remember.*

Outside, at the center of the courtyard, is a huge brown cylinder, shaped like a crematory urn, bearing the names of the death camps and of the Warsaw ghetto.

Inside the building is the crypt, the main feature of the Memorial. Raised above the floor is a symbolic tomb of black marble, in the shape of the Shield of David. Light falls upon it from the glass dome overhead. A perpetual flame burns at its center. In the Tomb are the ashes of martyrs collected from the death camps at Auschwitz, Belsen, Chelmno, Maidaneck, Mauthausen, Sobibor, and Treblinka, as well as from the ruins of the Warsaw ghetto. Here also are kept the parchment registers describing the sufferings and the martyrdom of the Jewish communities of Europe wiped out by the Nazis.

The wall behind the crypt bears a Hebrew inscription from Lamentations: "Look, all of you, and see if there be any agony like unto my agony; young and old, my maidens and my young men have been slaughtered."

The building also contains a Hall of Remembrance where are kept Memorial Books which preserve the names of martyrs, the library and archives of the Center of Contemporary Documentation of Nazi Atrocities, various departments, and a museum housing permanent and transient exhibits dealing with the holocaust.

Shrine of the Book at Jerusalem Museum

Interior of Shrine

The National Jewish Museum in Israel

1965

The Israel National Museum was dedicated in 1965. It is built on
a hill in the geographical, governmental, and educational center
of Jerusalem. It is surrounded by the new Knesset (Parliament)
building, the Israel ministries, the campus of the Hebrew University,
and the crusaders' Monastery of the Cross. From its site one is
afforded a magnificent panorama of the city.

The Museum brings together under one roof the Biblical and
Archaeological Museum, housing an outstanding collection of
precious antiquities excavated in the Holy Land and the Near East;
the Bezalel National Art Museum; the Shrine of the Book housing
the priceless Dead Sea Scrolls and other invaluable findings of the
Judean desert; and an Art Garden which comprises a magnificent
collection of modern sculpture.

Particularly striking is the Shrine of the Book. It is white domed,
set off by a black-basalt wall which suggests the constant struggle
between good and evil (theme of the Scroll of the War between the
Sons of Light and the Sons of Darkness), as well as the sufferings
of the Jews over a period of two millennia.

The precious scrolls are kept in an underground chamber reached
through a tunnel. Also displayed therein are the Bar Kokhba Letters
and the documents and relics from Masada.

A separate section of the Museum is built to recreate the rough-
stone appearance of the Dead Sea caves where are displayed in their
simulated natural setting, the various artifacts found in them, such
as textiles, glass, bronze, and wooden vessels.

Jewish Museum

Yivo Institute

The Jewish Museum in New York

1948-1965

On Fifth Avenue and Ninety-Second Street on what may be called "Museum Row"—a few blocks away from the Metropolitan Museum of Art, the Yiddish Scientific Institute (YIVO), the Guggenheim Museum and others—is located the Jewish Museum of the Jewish Theological Seminary of America. There were several landmarks in the history of the Museum. Its foundations were laid in 1904 in a small room in the library of the old Seminary building. The collection kept growing until in 1948, through a gift of the Warburg family mansion by Mrs. Felix Warburg, it was opened to the public as the Jewish Museum of New York. In 1965 a new wing was added on the side facing Fifth Avenue, which now serves as the main entrance instead of Ninety-Second Street, as theretofore.

The Museum houses many historical treasures. Among these are the thirteenth century ark from Cairo (see p. 82), a sixteenth century faience mosaic synagogue wall from Persia, rare shofars, variously shaped havdalah spice boxes, antique kiddush cups, silver Purim greggers (noisemakers), ancient artistic marriage contracts, elaborate collection of medals and plaques, struck in honor of Jews who made notable contributions to Judaism and to civilization.

The YIVO Library and Archives on Fifth Avenue and Eighty-Sixth Street in New York City contain a rich, colorful repository of materials on Jewish life, past and present. They comprise varied demographic data, labor movements, diverse documents on the story of Yiddish throughout the ages, voluminous materials of Nazi chronicles, accounts of survivors of Hitlerism, historical photographs, Jewish music, plays, posters of all kinds—a vast collection of some 2,000,000 items which are constantly being augmented.